with love and admiration

Uncle Fred

Merry Christmas
2022

WINNING THE WAR THROUGH PRAYER

Spiritual Warfare Praying

C. Fred Dickason, Th. D.

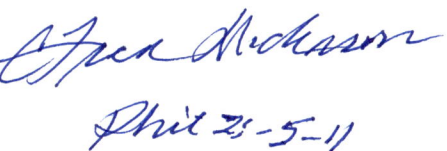

Phil 2:5-11

WESTBOW
PRESS
A DIVISION OF THOMAS NELSON
& ZONDERVAN

Copyright © 2016 C. Fred Dickason, Th. D.

All rights reserved. No part of this book may be used or reproduced by any means, graphic, electronic, or mechanical, including photocopying, recording, taping or by any information storage retrieval system without the written permission of the author except in the case of brief quotations embodied in critical articles and reviews.

Scripture quotations taken from the New American Standard Bible® (NASB), Copyright © 1960, 1962, 1963, 1968, 1971, 1972, 1973, 1975, 1977, 1995 by The Lockman Foundation
Used by permission. www.Lockman.org

WestBow Press books may be ordered through booksellers or by contacting:

WestBow Press
A Division of Thomas Nelson & Zondervan
1663 Liberty Drive
Bloomington, IN 47403
www.westbowpress.com
1 (866) 928-1240

Because of the dynamic nature of the Internet, any web addresses or links contained in this book may have changed since publication and may no longer be valid. The views expressed in this work are solely those of the author and do not necessarily reflect the views of the publisher, and the publisher hereby disclaims any responsibility for them.

Any people depicted in stock imagery provided by Thinkstock are models, and such images are being used for illustrative purposes only. Certain stock imagery © Thinkstock.

ISBN: 978-1-5127-5980-8 (sc)
ISBN: 978-1-5127-5982-2 (hc)
ISBN: 978-1-5127-5981-5 (e)

Library of Congress Control Number: 2016916592

Print information available on the last page.

WestBow Press rev. date: 10/24/2016

CONTENTS

Prologue ix
Preface xi
Introduction xv

Part I
Biblical Perspectives on Spiritual Warfare

Chapter 1 Reality and Resources in Spiritual Warfare 1
   The Reality of Spiritual Warfare 3
      The Enemy's Personnel 3
      The Enemy's Plan 7
   Our Resources in Spiritual Warfare 8
      The Power of the Lord 8
      The Provision of God's Armor 10
      Effective Use of the Armor 13
   Our Response to Spiritual Warfare 15

Chapter 2 The Place of Prayer in Spiritual Warfare 19
   Prayer recognizes Christ's authority. 20
      The Sovereign Authority of Christ 20
      Our Delegated Authority 21
   Prayer Relies on Christ's Intervention 22
      We are helpless in the battle 22
      We are hopeful in the battle 23
   Prayer relieves human needs 24
      God supplies our physical needs 24
      God provides for spiritual deliverance 25

Prayer realizes victory in spiritual warfare 26
God keeps us alert 26
God brings justice 27
God delivers His own 28

Chapter 3 Spiritual Warfare Battle Tactics 30
Our Prayer Defense 32
Defense by the Savior's Prayers 32
Defense by the Saint's Prayers 33
Our Prayer Offense 40
Against Evil Influences in Governments 41
Against Evil Influences in Society 42
Our Responsibility 47

Chapter 4 Spiritual Warfare Objectives 49
Winning Persons to Christ 50
Problems to Overcome 50
Prayer that Overcomes 52
Building Persons in Christ 54
Standing in Assurance 54
Protection from False Doctrine and Life Style 55
Freeing Persons from Demonic Bondage 63
Reasons for Bondage 63
Relief from Bondage 66

Chapter 5 Practical Pointers in Spiritual Warfare 69
Preparedness for the Battle 70
Alertness 71
Allegiance 72
Perspectives for the Battle 75
Reality Check 75
Balance Check 78
Hope Check 79

Part II
Pattern Warfare Prayers

Chapter 6 Psalms for Warfare 86

Chapter 7 Prayers for Personal Freedom 90
    Recognizing the Reality of Spiritual Warfare 90
    Protection from the Forces of Evil 91
    Freedom from Demonic and Occult Bondage 92

Chapter 8 Prayer for Personal Needs 104
    Prayer for the Filling of the Holy Spirit 104
    Prayer for the Salvation of Others 105
    Prayer for Physical Healing 106
    Prayer for Marriages and Families 107
    For Marriages in Trouble 107
    For Troubled or Rebellious Children 108
    For Problems with Addictions 108
    Prayer against Sexual Perversions 109
    Prayer against Pornography 110
    Prayer against Self-Stimulation 111
    Prayer for the Workplace 112
    Prayer Regarding the Possible Gift of Tongues 113
    Prayer against Passivity 113
    Prayer against House Haunting 114
    Prayer for Dedicating a House or Building 115
    Prayer for Spiritual Welfare of Children 115

Chapter 9 Prayer for Church and Missions 118
    Prayer for Revival in the Local Church 118
    Prayer for Pastors and Missionaries 120
    Prayer against False Religions 121

Chapter 10 Prayer for Our Country and the World 122
    Prayer for Our Country 122
    Prayer regarding Human Trafficking 123
    Prayer for Our Educational System 124
    Prayer for Christian Education 124
    Prayer for Governmental Leaders 125
    Prayer for Defeat of Ungodly Movements 125
    Prayer against Terrorism 126
    Prayer for Truth in Media 127
    Prayer for Suffering Christians 127
    Prayer for the Persecuted Church 128
    Prayer against Witchcraft and Satanism 128
    Prayer for Peace 129

Selected Brief Bibliography 131
Organizations That Promote Spiritual Warfare Prayer 133

PROLOGUE

Remember the "ice bucket challenge" when people poured a pail of ice water over their heads to raise awareness and funds for the fight against ALS? I didn't take the challenge, because I felt I could just visualize what the experience would be like; and for me that was sufficient!

Winning the War through Prayer is like a bucket of cold water thrown onto a largely lukewarm Church. For those who have already experienced the power of demonic forces and the triumph of Christ, this book will give them more practical knowledge of how to confront our enemy. For those who have ignored the biblical teaching about our invisible war, such readers will be jolted into reality. Their eyes will be open to a new level of spiritual discernment and a new way of praying that is directed against the forces that seek to destroy us. And, best of all, no matter where we are in our walk with Christ, all of us---me included---benefit from this book's insight and wisdom.

I have known Fred Dickason for more than 35 years. We served together on the faculty of Moody Bible Institute back in the late 1970's. Already then Fred was meeting with people who had clear signs of demonic oppression who came to him for counsel and help. After I became the pastor of The Moody Church, on at least a few occasions, Fred and I met to counsel those who were troubled by evil spirits and showed clear evidence of demonic invasion or harassment. I respect Fred's knowledge of spiritual warfare and the insights God has given him to bring clarity to a subject that is often overlooked or misunderstood.

Not everyone agrees with every detail of Fred's views. Those who take the point of view that Christians are protected from spiritual attacks such as demonic invasion disagree with his direct confrontation of evil spirits. But Fred believes that when there is occultism in a family or when Christians dabble in some for of occult activity, evil spirits take advantage of these inroads. The enemy can also use childhood trauma, sexual abuse, and other kinds of victimization to gain a spiritual foothold in someone's life. We as a staff here at The Moody Church have certainly encountered people who have been victims of Satan's evil schemes, and through direct confrontation of the enemy they have experienced the freedom Jesus offers.

No one is an expert in dealing with the spirit world. But Fred, perhaps more than anyone else I know, has had a forty year track record of helping those who have been bound by the devil to experience deliverance through Christ. We would be foolish to not take advantage of his wisdom and insights.

Whether or not you have taken the ice bucket challenge, read this book and like me you will experience a wakeup call that will remind you that we have an enemy who seeks our destruction and a Savior who delivers all who believe in Him. You will have a better understanding of why some Christians are continually defeated and the path that points to victory and eventual triumph.

This is a handbook on spiritual warfare. No frills, just the facts, just reality and just a blueprint for spiritual freedom for us and those we seek to help. Read it once, read it twice, and learn to pray to win the battle.

Dr. Erwin W. Lutzer
Senior Pastor, Emeritus
The Moody Church, Chicago

PREFACE

Why another book on spiritual warfare? Aren't there enough? What else do we need to know?

Good questions! But there is a good answer.

How many of you have read a book that focuses on the place and the particulars of pointed prayer for the battle? Well, that's what this book is all about. In my experience and exposure to the actual facts, Christians do not understand what can be done in spiritual warfare praying. They don't know beyond a simple general petition what to pray for and what to pray against. Our Western world view does not open our minds to letting us think of how we face a worldwide demonic opposition to biblical truth and faith. God is up there, and we are down here; and there is very little activity from the spirit world. Why pray about something that is not relevant to our thinking? And what is there to pray about? We pray our usual prayers; are they not sufficient?

I spent fourteen Wednesdays speaking on spiritual warfare praying to a prayer meeting group in a conservative Bible believing church. At a second such church, I gave fifteen lessons on the same subject. Neither church seemed to catch on! No one incorporated the principles clearly set before them from the biblically based messages on how to pray effectively for Christian life, ministry, and missions. It did not register and did not change their ingrained pattern of "Be with these folks and them with health and strength and give them fruit for their ministry." There was no recognition of the spiritual battle facing individuals, the church, and missionaries. They were comfortable with their routine praying as was their custom.

We need to get real! We need to realize what world shaking evil programs and events keep going on around us. We need to realize how the spirit world affects us, our children, and our community. We need to recognize what formidable and tragic needs there are. What is going on in the spirit world, and how does it affect the Christian and the church and its mission?

That's why I am writing this book. After over fifty years of Bible teaching and over forty years of spiritual warfare counseling, I write with knowledgeable concern. I write with a biblical world view and orientation to those who need to face up to the war and to our opportunity to carry on the Great Commission of making disciples. We need instruction found in the Bible about the reality of the spiritual war in which every believer is engaged. Some are aware of the war, and others drift on as if it is unreal. Even those who recognize some of this reality do not take practical steps to investigate how to pray and how to deal with the spiritual war that is going on around us.

Let me share with you some insights and applications that the Lord has brought to those of us who treat those in need. I am thankful for those who are informed and dedicated to prayer and to counseling who want answers to pressing needs. There are good biblically based organizations that promote biblical counseling and meaningful prayer.

How do you pray against Satan's inroads into your church, your business, your family? How do we pray for our missionaries who face demonic opposition? How do we handle ghostly appearances? What about house hauntings, pressures on the body, emotional stresses, and sudden suicidal or murderous thought?

What place does prayer have in spiritual warfare? Against what demonic tactics should we be praying? What practical tactics and objectives could we incorporate? What cautions should we observe?

I hope that this brief survey might stimulate us to approach seriously the urgent matter of praying for victory---to winning the war through prayer. God is in charge. He is sovereign. He has provided in Christ what we need to know and the authority to carry on the program of our victorious and worthy Savior.

INTRODUCTION

Winning the War through Prayer

Did you know that the moment you trusted the Lord Jesus as your Savior you stepped onto the battle field? Well you did! And you are in danger. Satan opposes God and His children at all times. He has well trained henchmen who are always ready and able to directly or indirectly to attack you. Jesus said He would build His church even though He was opposed by the authorities (gates) of the unseen world of spirits. We need supernatural help!

But the Lord did not leave us without intelligence reports and resources in the battle. Would you like to know more about this? Read on! Learn about your enemies, their power, and their schemes. Learn also of the power of the Lord and your line of communication in spiritual warfare praying

God has established prayer for many purposes. Basically, it is our way of fellowshipping with Him. In prayer we worship and praise our Triune God. We give Him thanks and express our love for Him. We commit our lives and our concerns to Him, asking for His grace, wisdom, and power to honor Him. In prayer we intercede for others and their needs. We pray for the extension of God's truth and His kingdom. We seek the expansion of the gospel and Christ's church.

Another important aspect found in the Bible is warfare praying. You can find such prayers in what are called the "imprecatory psalms." These call for God's justice to intervene, to relieve, and to judge God's enemies. A great percentage of the psalms express such prayer. Though not as frequent in the New Testament, there are prayers for God's protection, intervention, relief, justice, and the furtherance of His purposes.

In this book entitled *Winning the War through Prayer,* I would like to call your attention to the spiritual warfare in which all Christians are engaged and to how to pray intelligently, pointedly, and biblically to gain victory in that warfare. I believe that God wants us to have the perspective and benefits He has provided in this biblical study. These studies build successively upon each other. Let's consider the following topics:

- Reality and Resources in Spiritual Warfare
- Place of Prayer in Spiritual Warfare
- Our Tactics in Spiritual Warfare Praying
- Our Objectives in Spiritual Warfare Praying
- Practical Pointers for Spiritual Warfare Praying
- Pattern Prayers for Specific Occasions

Note: All quotations of Scripture are taken from the NASB unless otherwise noted.

PART I

Biblical Perspectives on Spiritual Warfare

CHAPTER 1

Reality and Resources in Spiritual Warfare

"Drive your car off this bridge when you reach the top!" Intruding words in her mind scared this middle-aged woman. She did not obey them, but she prayed against such thoughts. She then sought my counsel. We found that demons had inserted these words into her mind. She came to understand that her mother had been involved in witchcraft and then in Satanism and that this had affected her.

Have you had strange, unwanted thoughts enter your mind? Have you heard of others who do? Voices may come from several sources. Some may have come from evil spirits. Hard to believe? Well it happens all the time to some people, and they don't know why or what to do with these thoughts. Such repeated thoughts can drive a person to distraction, to depression, or even to suicide.

Your mind is a marvelous creation! It is the citadel of your soul, and there is a battle for the control of it. For ages Satan and his demons have been very successful in seeking to control the minds of unbelievers and believers alike. They have propagandized and influenced individuals, societies, and governments. We need to guard our minds by standing firm in the truth of the Word of God. We are responsible for evaluating the thoughts that enter our minds.

The Bible leads us to understand that the mind is different from the brain. The brain is material part of the body; the mind is immaterial or spiritual. God created the first man from the dust (Heb., *aphar*) of the ground (Heb., *adamah*). This is the material part---the body. God breathed into him the breath of life (Heb., *ruach*). This was the first person's spiritual part. This is the mind that allowed him to think and feel and choose with God. This is the image of God in humanity. The whole of a person, including mind and body, is called soul or being (Heb., *nephesh*). Each of us is (not has) a living soul composed of body and spirit (Gen. 2:7). Our being---our person---reflects God's person.

Our spiritual well-being depends on the condition and state of our minds. Whatever controls our minds controls us. God knows the importance of our minds. We know---at least in part---the importance of our minds. Satan and his demons know the importance of our minds, and they are constantly seeking to gain control of our minds. He wants to take the place of God in our thinking, and he wants to control our minds---not to cultivate as would God but to deceive and to destroy our effectiveness for Christ.

Listen to what the Spirit of God said through the Apostle Paul in Ephesians 6:10--18. Here God is warning us against the mind-control purposes and techniques of the devil. Satan is waging warfare for our minds and the minds of our children. We need to know how to pray in the face of this battle.

If we are to live successful and unshackled Christian lives and train our children to live free from Satan's attempts to control our minds, we must recognize the reality of spiritual warfare and rely upon the resources provided by our risen Lord Jesus Christ. What must we know? What must we do to stand successfully in the battle and gain the victory for ourselves and for our children? What must we do to honor our Lord Jesus?

First, we must know what the Bible teaches about the reality of spiritual warfare. So let's take a brief survey of the Bible's teaching on this subject.

The Reality of Spiritual Warfare

The Enemy's Personnel (Eph. 6:10--12)

Listen to the important final words of the letter of Paul in Ephesians 6:10--12 (NASB):

> Finally, be strong in the Lord, and in the strength of His might. Put on the full armor of God, that you may be able to stand firm against the schemes of the devil. For our struggle is not against flesh and blood, but against the rulers, against the powers, against the world forces of this darkness, against the spiritual forces of wickedness in the heavenly places.

We need to understand what enemies we face. The name devil means slanderer. His other name, Satan, means adversary. He hates and battles against God and His people. We are his targets. We should know our enemy, so God has informed us through his Word.

God originally created Satan as the mighty angel Lucifer and appointed him as the head of God's honor guard (Isa. 14:12--14; Ezek. 28:14--16). Satan became occupied with his beauty and position desired more for himself and rebelled against his Creator. He desired to rule over all and enticed many (perhaps as many as one- third of the angels to follow his opposition to God (Rev. 12:3—4). We should know about our enemies if we are to pray and act against them.

Reality of Satan

In the Old Testament, there is ample evidence that Satan is a real person with evil nature and evil intent. The Lord Jesus said that devil---another name for Satan---was a liar and murderer from the beginning (John 8:44). This is a clear reference to the temptation of Adam and Eve in the beginning of the human race. We read in Genesis 3 that Satan by speaking through a serpent cast doubt upon God's character and word. That this refers to Satan himself is substantiated by Revelation 12:9 where Satan is called "the serpent of old."

In the book of Ezekiel, God describes Satan as "the anointed cherub who guards," (Ezek. 28:14, 16). The cherubim are a high order of created angelic beings. Satan is of the highest orders of angelic beings. He is very intelligent and powerful. Humans are no a match for him. We are told to be alert, to guard ourselves, and to rely on the Lord's power to resist the devil.

Rebellion of Satan

In Ezekiel 28:15, 17--18, the prophet Ezekiel describes Satan: "You were blameless in your ways from the day you were created until unrighteousness was found in you . . . Your heart was lifted up because of your beauty . . . Therefore I have brought fire from the midst of you; it has consumed you." Satan's pride led him to desire more for himself than God had granted in creating him (1 Tim. 3:6). So God judged him by casting him out of heaven.

Isaiah 14:12--15 speaks of Satan as "star of the morning, son of the dawn." His manifesto is stated in five times by "I will." He would ascend above God to rule as "the Most High" (Heb., *El Elyon*). For him control is the name of the game leading to power and glory. But God has cast him down in judgment.

Some tragedies might seem just natural; but from one of the earliest books of the Old Testament, we read of what went on behind the scenes with Job's sufferings (Job 1--2). God challenged Satan and the battle field was Job's mind and body. Satan insulted God saying that Job honored God only because God was good to him. Satan claims that Job honored God for His gifts and protection and not for His wonderful person. God won the battle and restored Job. But the whole story lets us know that Satan was well known in the early history of the Old Testament.

In the New Testament, nineteen of the twenty seven books mention Satan by one of his names. Christ is responsible for twenty five of the twenty nine of his mentions in the gospels. Every writer of the New Testament mentions him. Satan is a real person, not just evil in general, an evil influence, or evil personified. Christ argued with him, reasoning from the Scriptures (Matt. 4:1--11). After successfully resisting him, Christ commanded him as a real person, "Begone, Satan!" Matthew records, "Then devil left Him; and behold, angels came and began to minister to Him" (Matt. 4:11).

We can read of Satan's rebellion described in Isaiah 14 with five statements of "I will." His fall from great position included his selling one-third of the angels his rebellious bill of goods (Rev. 12:4). Ezekiel speaks of his enticing others to rebel with him against the Most High God. "By the abundance of your trade you were internally filled with violence, and you sinned . . . By the multitude of your iniquities, in the unrighteousness of your trade, you profaned your sanctuaries" (Ezek. 28:16, 18). How insanely proud to imagine that those few creatures could overcome their creator!

Reality of Demons

You might wonder how a creature like the devil can affect so many people and places. Well, he has help. He is personally limited, but the angels that fell with him are now "his angels." He needs all the help he can get, for he is fighting a lost cause; and Christ will cast all of them into the lake of fire (Matt. 25:41).

There are more than one hundred references in the New Testament to demons. The term *daimonion* is used sixty-three times, and *pneumata* (spirits) is used forty-three times when referring to Satan's angels. Christ claimed authority over them and cast them out of demonized persons to prove his messiahship. At least nine demonized cases are treated in detail in the gospels. There are seventeen mentions of demonization in the gospels and four in Acts. Demons are real, and they really oppress humans.

Ranks of Demons (Eph. 6:12; Col. 1:16)

God is a God of order and organization. He created ranks of angels as in a military organization. The term "host of angels" refers to an army of angels. Demons, as fallen angels---the only Biblical identity of demons---are well organized in order of the following ranks rather consistently in Scripture: thrones, dominions, principalities, powers, and spirits. There are other authorities as well. World rulers govern national or local territories. Such were the "Prince of Persia" and the "Prince of Greece" (Dan. 10:20).

Nature of Demons

Demons are fallen angels. They are associated with the devil in several places as "his angels" (Matt. 25:41; Rev. 12:4, 7). Though created good, they defected with Lucifer (the Shining One) and became evil. Just as angels, they are spirit beings, having no body (Heb. 1:14). They were created persons with intellect, emotions, and will. They were able to willfully desire to rule with Satan, and ultimately they chose to rebel with him. They are now morally perverted, indicated by such terms as "unclean spirit" (Matt. 12:43), "evil spirits" (Luke 7:21), or "spiritual forces of wickedness" (Eph. 6:12). They are bent on doing harm to God and His people. They retain great powers but are limited by God and answerable to God. They shall be judged and cast into the Lake of Fire---the final place for Satan's angels and human unbelievers.

The Enemy's Plan (Eph. 6:11; 2 Cor. 2:11)

Satan's Schemes

We will treat this in more detail in the next chapters. At this point, it is sufficient to note these over all points to give perspective. He opposes God's person and program. This is obvious right from the beginning and he continues until the future when God judges him (Gen. 3; Rev. 12:7; 20:17--19). He attacks and deceives mankind. He blinds the minds of unsaved mankind so that they may not hear and understand the gospel of Christ and His salvation. Paul states, "the god of this world has blinded the minds of the unbelieving, that they might not see the light of the gospel of the glory of Christ, who is the image of God" (2 Cor. 4:4). Satan delights in torment and destruction, causing suffering and death (Rev. 2:10; 9:5, 11). He attacks and seeks to destroy God's children (1 Chron. 21:1; Acts 5:3). He leads persons to sin and to incur the discipline of God. He leads humans into sinful life styles that ruin health, promote false religions, and pervert sexuality (Rom. 1:21--32).

Satan's Goals

Ultimately Satan seeks these ends. He would overthrow God's person and take control ("I will make myself like the Most High" (Heb., *El Elyon,* Isa. 14:12). The Antichrist of the last days will be one of Satan's final attempts at turning mankind into rebels like himself (2 Thess. 2:8--9; Rev. 12, 13).

Satan would thwart God's plan of salvation and kingdom. He keeps humans from understanding the message of Christ and sows false religionists (Matt. 13:24--30). He blinds the minds (the intellect and emotions) of the unsaved so that they cannot see the truth in Christ (2 Cor. 4:5--6). He seeks to ruin God's people and their effective witness to truth by persecution and fear (1 Pet. 5:8--9; Rev. 2:10).

If we are aware of these schemes of the enemy, we can be alert to his approach, resist him in the authority and strength of the Lord, and pray effectively against him.

Our Resources in Spiritual Warfare

The Power of the Lord (Eph. 6:10)

In the midst of the battle, we must remember that we have God's resources at our disposal; and we must avail ourselves of them if we are to win the immediate skirmish. God has supplied us sufficient resources, and God is Himself the all wise and all powerful protector and director of His soldiers. Through the Lord Jesus and our union with Him, we can stand firm in the fray. Remember three very important facts that God has revealed. As we live and as we pray we must keep these truths in mind.

God is the sovereign ruler of the universe (Isa. 40:28--31; 43:11--13).

Our God and Father, the Father of our Lord Jesus Christ, is the eternal, self-existent, self-sufficient, unchanging living God with whom there is no rival whatsoever! "He gives strength to the weary and to him who lacks might he increases power" (Isa. 40:29). He needs no advice or help from any creature. He grants new strength to those who trust Him. He rules over all, there is no god beside Him. "And there is none who can deliver out of My hand. I act and who can reverse it" (43:11, 13). He does whatever He pleases in heaven and on earth (Ps 135:6). "The LORD (Heb., *Yahweh*) has established His throne in the heavens; and His sovereignty rules over all" (the universe, Ps. 103:19). The one who has trusted Christ as his Savior is joined to Him. That person has nothing to fear and will never be forsaken (Heb. 13:5--6)!

Christ created all things material and spiritual---including all angels (Col. 1:16).

Paul wrote to assure the believers in Colossae that the Son of God was over all the spirits they feared and had previously served. They did not need to wonder if they would be troubled by those principalities and powers upon whom they depended for safety and provision. The Christ they were now trusting was far above these created spirit beings who were regarded by the pagans as actual gods in charge of all of life. The Risen Christ was the creator of all material things and spiritual beings. They were created by Him and for Him and must answer to Him. Now the believers were joined in life to the Living Son of God. "For He delivered us from the domain of darkness, and transferred us to the kingdom of His beloved Son" (Col. 1:13). They would be safe in following Him. And so will we as we depend upon Him.

Christ has all authority and power in heaven and earth (Matt. 28:18).

In giving His Great Commission, the Risen Christ assured His disciples that He would back them up with the total authority He has received from His Father. It was given to Him, and He delegated authority to His disciples. He has intrinsic and total authority, and He has provided sufficient authority to the believer to carry out His commission to make disciples and to face their enemies. Christ's authority extends not only to earth but also to the heavens. That includes all humans and all angels, good and evil. In the ongoing battle between evil and righteousness, believers have the support of the risen and authoritative God-man. With donated authority from the risen Christ we can face our supernatural foes.

The Provision of God's Armor (Eph. 6:12--17)

As a wise commanding general the Lord has not sent His soldiers into battle without the firepower of His authority. We have spoken of Christ's power and His delegating to us sufficient authority. Neither does He send us into battle without sufficient protection. We have the overall armor of God that is sufficient to protect us in the ongoing battle.

While the apostle Paul was in house arrest, there were Roman soldiers standing guard outside. In writing to the Ephesians of spiritual warfare, he noted the pieces of armor on the soldier and remembered mentions of the armor of God in the Older Testament found in Isaiah 59:16--18 and Psalm 18:30--35. Putting this together he described what God has provided for His believer-warriors for the spiritual warfare we face.

Today's solders are trained to know their weapons inside and out. They are even trained to dismantle and reassemble their weapons in the dark. This is important for their survival and the survival of their fellow soldiers.

There are six pieces of armor described in Ephesians 6:12--17. It is important to distinguish properly what sort they are and to describe them accurately so that we are acquainted with the weaponry and know how to use it. It is necessary for our spiritual well-being and for our fellow believer-warriors. I believe that there are two categories of weapons and that their identity is rather clear. This seems to be indicated by the text and by the nature of the armament.

Three Pieces Already on Due to The Believer's Position in Christ

By position in Christ I am referring to the grace gift of a perfect standing granted us the very moment we personally receive Christ as Savior---including total forgiveness and justification. These pieces of armor are already ours in believing Him.

Belt of Truth. This is the truth in Christ, not referring to our personal truthfulness. That is what the enemy make us doubt. Christ is the way, the truth, and the life. Truth is centered in Him, the truth of our relationship to God in our salvation. We are in the truth system, and we need not seek the truth about God and ourselves in any other religion or philosophy. The belt on the Roman soldier held his garments together and out of the way and supported his back in the strain of battle. It also held his short sword---a great offensive weapon.

When evil forces seek to make us question the sufficiency of Christ for our salvation and defense, we must remember that we are supported by God in His truth system. We are secure!

Breastplate of Righteousness. The Roman soldier wore around his chest and thorax a great protective device. It could be of metal or of leather with metal pieces sown together like scales on a fish. It was effective in stopping or minimizing the penetration of a sword, arrow, or spear. The Christian's breastplate is that of the righteousness of Christ---the righteousness that comes from God through justification by faith. This is an unchanging right standing before God. It is not our own righteous behavior. That would be inadequate for defense in the battle. When Satan or demons accuse us (Rev. 12:10) we can depend upon our eternal righteousness of Christ. We can know that God is for us and that no one can assail successfully our standing before God (Rom. 8:33--34).

Shoes of Peace. We need non-slip boots in the midst of the battle. The Roman soldier had hobnail sandals laced up over his calves. This assured good footing while engaged in conflict while carrying the heavy shield and sword. God has declared that we have settled peace with Him through the blood of the cross. He is for us not against us when we run into conflict with the enemy. This grants us confidence in our non-slip relationship with God even in the midst of the battle.

Three Pieces to Put on in the Believer's Practice in the Lord

The text indicates a change to the type of weaponry we must now pick up. "In addition to all (of the above armor), taking up . . ." This calls for action on our part.

Shield of Faith. With this piece we can ward off the firery darts of the devil. We must exercise confidence in God and His Word. God is for us so that no one can be successfully against us if we raise the shield of faith. We can stop and dismiss the deadly lies of the enemy as he would make us doubt God's goodness and power to deliver. He would even make us doubt our faith in Christ. He would tell us that we are totally inadequate for the battle and that we have no power to resist. LIES! By faith we trust God to take care of us in the heat of the battle!

Helmet of Salvation. Donning this piece grants us the mindset that we are on the winning side and will experience God's deliverance in the battle. The word salvation has as its basic meaning "deliverance." Its connotation depends upon the context. The context in this case is the battle with the enemy. So it refers to deliverance from the foes in the struggle. A similar use of this word is found in 1 Thessalonians 5:8 where the helmet is called the "hope of salvation." This hope is the certainty that we are on the winning side in the war We should have no place for doubt. We shall overcome as we depend upon our Risen and conquering Savior!

Sword of the Spirit. This is the major offensive weapon. It is the word of God---not the general message of the Bible but the specific sayings of the Bible that fit the situation that we face (Gr., *rhema* not *logos*). This is the idea in the Greek word *rhema* which refers not to someone's spoken word, but to God's spoken word. Note how appropriately the Lord Jesus' used the sayings of Deuteronomy as they fit the temptations of the devil. He lived by God's specific commands (Matt. 4:4--11). The devil tempted Christ to turn stone into bread to satisfy His hunger. Christ appropriately quoted God's Word, "Man does not live on bread alone, but on every word that proceeds out of the mouth of God" (Deut. 8:3). We must know the Word of God and how to use it if we are to attack the temptations of the evil one!

Effective Use of the Armor

Proper Definition of the Armor

An improper understanding of these provisions will confuse and defeat us. We must distinguish position and practice aspects. It would be disheartening to think that we had to develop such righteousness that could defend us from the devil. So also if it were our peace of heart that defended us, we could be open to defeat; because we did not have peace within. Likewise, as to the belt of truth, our truthfulness is not to be confused with God's truth in Christ.

We must not confuse proper and popular concepts. To think that the helmet of deliverance is the piece that is designed to guard our minds is to miss the concept that we are on the winning side. Notice that all the pieces of armor---not just the helmet---are designed to guard our minds. A proper understanding of these provisions will enlighten us and help us. We can take a firm stand in the truth against the enemy. We can take a confident approach to victory.

Proper Donning of the Armor

How shall we put on the armor of God? There are different opinions. Consider the following suggestions.
Putting on the Armor Granted Due to Our Position. There is a parallel with what Romans 6 says about our victory over our sin nature. There we are to reckon ourselves dead to sin and alive to God and then to present our members as instruments of warfare to God for His use. So with the positional armor, we are to (1) reckon that

we have that armor already on, (2) thank God for its provision, and (3) advance in the battle in this realization and confidence.

Putting on the Armor Given for Our Practice. The command, "In addition, taking up" indicates an action required on our part. The nature of the armor suggests that these are related to our faith and obedience to be prepared for the battle. So in obedience to God, we are to (1) recognize our personal needs these pieces suggest, (2) bolster our armor by knowing God's truth involved, and (3) pray with thanks for their provision and that God would enable us to put them on and keep them on in the battle.

God has given us all the armor we need to stand in the battle and to gain the victory through our relationship with God. We need not fear the battle, for He is by our side.

The Prayer of Believers (Eph. 6:18--19)

We will develop this matter of prayer in more detail in the next chapters. But notice at this point that the apostle Paul tops off these six pieces of armor with prayer, the line of communication we have at all times. I have a friend who was the radio man just south of the battle of the bulge in WW II. He was key in calling in artillery strikes and in receiving orders from his commander. Just as the soldiers up front make radio contact with the artillery or airstrikes as backup, we have constant contact with the Captain of our salvation, the Lord Jesus, to call on Him for his backing in the battle.

Nothing is insignificant to the Lord Jesus. He cares for us. So Peter tells us, "casting all your anxiety upon Him, because He cares for you" (1Peter 5:7). There are many things we don't consider to be connected to spiritual warfare; but we need to remember that we wrestle not just with humans entities and human problems but with spiritual forces aligned against Christ and against us locally and worldwide (Eph 6:12).

Praying at All Times

We must call on the Lord at all times in the Spirit and be alert with all perseverance and petition for all the saints who are also in the battle (Eph. 6:18--19). The Ephesians, who lived formerly in constant fear of lesser deities (demon spirits connected with false gods), needed to know that the Sovereign Lord Jesus would back believers in the battle. These were the people who formerly depended upon their magic books and their enchantments to protect them. When they trusted Christ, they burned their magic books worth 137 man-year wages (Act. 19:18-20). They had to learn to depend upon the Lord. So must we! We are helpless in ourselves against such a formidable army of evil spirits, but with the Sovereign Risen Lord on our side we are more than victors! We must keep our lines of communication with our fire power open and active.

Our Response to Spiritual Warfare

There are some very practical steps we can take in reacting to the reality and danger of spiritual warfare that threatens our lives, that of our families, and the life of the Church of Christ.

Recognize the enemy's tactics

We must not be caught unaware. General Douglas MacArthur, Commander of US forces in the Pacific in WW II, declared, "The most important thing in battle is to know the enemy's plans." A military force must have its own plans; but if caught unaware by the enemy's tactics and attacks, it can be surprised and suffer tragic defeat. We used to sing, "Just remember Pearl Harbor!" We must remember that Satan has well thought-out and inclusive tactics and seeks to outwit us (Eph. 6:11).

Remember Christ's victory

We must keep in mind that the cross of Christ ruined Satan's power and rule. Through death the Lord judged Satan's domination of the world and granted freedom to those who trust Christ (Heb. 2:14--15). Christ's victory is described as stripping the enemy of his weapons, putting him to open shame, and parading his defeated forces in a victory march. When a conquering general invaded a stronghold city, he would first strip the defending soldiers of their weapons. Then he would rope or chain them one to another and parade them through the city showing the people that they should never trust these soldiers again. The conquering general was in charge (Col. 2:15). And so it is with Christ. We can trust him as the victorious ruler of God's choice.

Rely on Christ's deliverance

Christ will intervene on our behalf. His power and wisdom are active on our behalf. His promises are true. We must trust Him and not rely upon own our strength or wisdom. Christ is the sovereign ruler of the universe (Eph. 6:10). He is the creator of all things material and spiritual (Col. 1:16). Our enemies owe their very existence to Him, and they must answer to Him. He has His own power and the agency of servant angels who minister to us believers who shall inherit final salvation (Heb. 1:14).

Resist in Christ's authority

Our authority over the enemy is due to our position in Christ. It is delegated authority and not absolute as is Christ's. It is ours by virtue of our having been crucified, raised, and seated with Christ in the heavenlies far above all opposing spiritual powers. God displayed His power in the Old Testament by His delivering the Hebrews from Egypt in the Exodus. In the New Testament the measure of God's power is demonstrated in the death, resurrection, and exaltation of Christ at God's right hand in glory far above all spirit beings including Satan and all his armies (Eph. 1:19-23). Those who have trusted Christ have been legally crucified, raised, and seated with Christ in the heavenlies and are in Christ far above all our enemies. We have authority in Christ to resist and win over demons in the battle (Eph. 2:5--6). Christ has commissioned us with all authority to carry on His work (Matt. 28:18--20).

Conclusion

If we are going to stand firm in the battle and win the day, we must know the truth about spiritual warfare. We cannot ignore its reality. We must recognize Satan's schemes and be alert to his approaches. We should not back away in fear; but we must allow the Lord to strengthen us, to defend us, and to cultivate our minds in the truth of God's Word and in fellowship with Him.

James 4:7 sets forth the proper order of commands. "Submit to God." It is only in allegiance to Christ and in surrender to His authority that we can even begin to stand in His power, grow in His grace, and expect victory in spiritual warfare. This is the prerequisite to the following commands. We cannot resist or succeed on our own.

"Resist the devil." We must be active, not just passively standing by while the battle rages. We must defend ourselves with the resources and armor that God supplies. We cannot ignore the spiritual aspect of human trials, opposition, and battles that we encounter. We must be aware of a biblical world-view of spiritual reality and demonic interaction with the human and material world. Without this recognition, active resistance, and offensive action we will not win the battle.

"And he will flee from you." This is the promised result. God stands behind His promises. We will eventually succeed if we avail ourselves of God's resources. Since we may partially submit and partially resist, there may be partial victory. We can learn in the process and gain helpful experience in the battle, but we must persist in dependence on our victorious Lord. Then we will gain the victory and the freedom Christ has provided.

Spiritual warfare is real. No Christian is exempt. We all need to recognize God's revelation of God regarding the real world around us and so face the foes in the strength and armor of God. If we do not, we shall fail and suffer the loss and hurt inflicted by the enemy. But if we do, we shall overcome to our good and to the glory of the Lord Jesus Christ, our Savior and Captain in the battle.

Questions to Ponder

1. Of what do you think humans are composed (how many parts)? How does our mind relate to our body and our brain?

2. What kind of beings are angels and demons? How may they affect the human mind and body?

3. What evidence do you have that angels and demons exist and enter into human life and experiences?

4. What are the believer's resources in spiritual warfare? What are the pieces of armor God provides?

5. Knowing that spiritual warfare exists, what should be my attitude and action?

CHAPTER 2

The Place of Prayer in Spiritual Warfare

We read of the first battle of the people of Israel in the Bible in Exodus 17:8--16. Joshua led the army of Israel against the Amalekites. Moses stood on the mountain and prayed with his staff lifted up in the authority of God. When he became weary, he sat down and two men, Aaron and Hur, held up his arms with the staff of his authority. The people of God prevailed as long as Moses prayed.

Note the place of prayer in the battle of Jehoshaphat with three invading nations (2 Chron. 20:6--12).

Hezekiah's prayer saved Israel from the invasion of Sennacherib, king of Assyria (2 Kings 18--19). God said, "For I will defend this city to save it for My servant David's sake.' Then it happened that night that the angel of the LORD went out, and struck 185,000 in the camp of the Assyrians; and when men rose early in the morning, behold, all of them were dead" (2 Kings 19:34--35).

It is not strange to those acquainted with Biblical history that at the end of Paul's exhortation on spiritual warfare he should urge his readers to pray (Eph. 6:18).

What place, therefore, does prayer play in the reality of spiritual warfare?

Prayer recognizes Christ's authority.

The Sovereign Authority of Christ

We have a Risen Savior who rules over all. By virtue of His character and position Christ is the sovereign of all humans and angels. Consider who He is. God proclaims, "Behold, I am the LORD, the God of all flesh; is anything too difficult for Me?" (Jer. 32:27).

Creator (Col 1:16) and Sustainer (Col. 1:17)

The Son of God created all things, visible (material) and invisible (spiritual). All spirit beings--- including Satan and all his hosts--- owe their existence to Him and are responsible to Him. He created them holy, but they rebelled against Him. Christ also keeps all living things alive and functioning--- even all our cells. All beings owe their continued existence to His sustaining power. Christ sustains all creation---material and spiritual. He is the God of the galaxies and of the genes and of all spirits.

Providential Controller (Heb. 1:3)

Christ bears all things along, directs the affairs of man and beast, and moves them in the direction of His choice. He provides for all and presides over all. Nothing escapes His detection or slips by His surveillance.

Unrivaled Lord (Isa. 45:22--23; Phil. 2: 9--11)

The Risen God-man is seated at the right hand of God in a position of authority over all.
There here is no one who can begin to compare with Him. He is genuine God and genuine man who rules from heaven and awaits

His return to reign on earth. All must answer to Him. He is the ultimate Judge. We can take comfort and encouragement in this truth.

Worthy of Our Obedience (Matt. 28:18--20)

The risen and exalted Christ commissioned believers to represent Him and preach His message to the whole world. He possesses all authority, and those who represent him must live and move under His authority. We must follow His directions and live in obedience to Him. Only in this way can we be successful and win in spiritual warfare.

Our Delegated Authority

God has not sent His ambassadors and soldiers into battle without His backing. Christ commanded us to pray in His name (John 16:23--24). There has been some confusion as to what this means. We must understand this command if we are to win the battle.

What This Does Not Mean

To pray in Christ's name is not a magical formula that demands response. This does not mean praying with fervency (though good). This does not require a special feeling to be effective.

What This Does Mean

We rely upon our personal position. We are in Christ and joined to Him by the Spirit's baptism the very moment we trust Christ to be our Savior. We have a personal spiritual union with Christ that cannot be dissolved. We have the privilege of coming to God in

Jesus' authority. We are responsible to ask according to His will. Besides this we can preach, pray, and command in Christ's authority.

Prayer Relies on Christ's Intervention

We are helpless in the battle

Human strength is not sufficient.

Do you ever feel weak and without help? That may be usual, but God comes to our rescue. Psalm 146:3 reads, "Do not trust in princes, in mortal man, in whom there is no salvation." David numbered his army to find his strength. Satan had moved him to trust in his human resources and not in the Living God (1 Chron. 21:1--7). God was displeased with this and reduced David's 1, 570, 000 fighting men by 70, 000. In the book of Acts 19:13--17, we read of two of the seven sons of a high priest who tried to exorcize demons by merely naming in magical fashion the name of the Lord Jesus whom Paul preached. It did not work. The demon declared, "I recognize Jesus, and I know about Paul, but who are you?" The demon overcame the two men and sent them scurrying, because they were not really believers in Christ. It is only those who are joined to Christ and in submission to Him who can successfully command demons. Not by human strength or wisdom do we overcome but by depending upon the power and wisdom of God (Ps. 44:3--8).

Human boldness is not sufficient.

After ten of the twelve spies sent to spy out the promised land brought back a negative report to which the Lord spoke his displeasure, some of Israel's warriors attempted to assault the land in their own strength and not in obedience to the Lord. They were unsuccessful---struck down; and the ten died by a plague. Only the two spies who gave a good report lived (Num 14:39--45). We must rely on the Lord only and pray with complete dependence on Him.

We are hopeful in the battle

Christ has promised to answer.

We are encouraged to come boldly to the throne of grace in any time of need. We are in great need in the spiritual war that we face. The Lord Jesus gave us this promise: "And whatever you ask in My name, that will I do, that the Father may be glorified in the Son" (John 14:13). But we must abide in His fellowship and ask in dependence on Him (John 15:7).

Christ will actually intervene in the battle.

When Peter was arrested and imprisoned---expecting execution just as James---the church made fervent prayer for him; and the Lord sent an angel to free him from the prison where he was chained between two soldiers. Peter was freed, but the guards were executed for their failure (Acts 12:1--19).

Julie (changed name) grew up with a mother who was into witchcraft and then into Satanism. Group members ritually abused her, and wicked spirits invaded her. This resulted in some serious psychological problems as well. She and her husband experienced a course in spiritual warfare counseling. Through persistent prayer and commands in the name of Christ, she was eventually released from the bondage. She and her husband who was very supportive in the counseling and praying are now ministering to the actors, actresses, and supporting members of the film industry in Hollywood. They understand the culture and conduct two Bible classes on two studio grounds. Unusual results in answer to concentrated prayer!

We must rely upon Christ alone in our warfare praying!

Prayer relieves human needs

God supplies our physical needs

Prayer brings healing.

Sometimes the cause of illness is personal sin, and it must be confessed. The prayer of elders along with ceremonial wiping with oil can be the occasion for forgiveness and healing of the sick (James 5:14--16).

Sometimes the cause is the enemy's affliction. Job's horrible condition and suffering was brought on by Satan. This was not without the Lord's permission and restrictions (Job 1--2). After the Lord had taught him and after Job humbled himself, God healed Job and also restored his erring friends (Job 42:1--9). God allowed Satan to cause the Apostle Paul a difficult malady, but God used this to teach Paul humility (2 Cor. 12:7). Sometimes the Lord uses illness to cause dependence on Him. After Paul petitioned the Lord three times about his "thorn in the flesh," the Lord answered him three times, "My grace is sufficient for you, for power is perfected in weakness" (2 Cor.12:8--10). To a Jew any word spoken three times is final and certain.

Prayer brings strength.

Because we are weak, we need support in the midst of the battle. King David faced the opposition of ungodly persons: "a band of violent men have sought my life." So he prayed, "Turn to me, and be gracious to me; oh, grant Thy strength to Thy servant" (Ps. 86:14--16). And Isaiah states that God "gives strength to the weary, and to him who lacks might He increases power. Though youths grow weary and tired, and vigorous young men stumble badly, yet those who wait for the LORD will gain new strength" (Isa. 40:29--31). We may pray for others as well as for ourselves in spiritual struggle. The enemy is formidable and very strong and has a great track record, but we have the Risen Lord Jesus to intervene for us.

God provides for spiritual deliverance

Prayer keeps us from temptation.

> The Lord warned his disciples, "Keep watching and praying that you may not enter into temptation; the spirit is willing, but the flesh is weak" (Matt. 26:41). Peter knew the experience of failure; and he warns us, "Be of sober spirit, and be on the alert. Your adversary, the devil, prowls about like a roaring lion, seeking someone to devour." We are to resist him in our firm stance of faith and in prayer (1 Peter 5:8--9). We may ask for God's protection and alertness.

Prayer delivers us from our adversaries.

> The enemy is real and he is cunning and powerful. We can depend upon God to come to our aid in the battle. David's prayer can be a pattern for our prayer. "Let not the oppressed return dishonored; let the afflicted and needy praise Thy name. Do arise, O God, and plead Thine own cause . . . Do not forget the voice of Thine adversaries" (Ps. 74:21--23).
>
> Even such a giant of the faith as the Apostle Paul asked for supporting prayer. "Finally, brethren, pray for us that the word of the Lord may spread rapidly and be glorified, just as it did also with you; and that we may be delivered from perverse and evil men, for not all have faith. But the Lord is faithful, and He will strengthen and protect you from the evil one" (2 Thess. 3:1--3). There is the hint that the enemy would retaliate against them for praying for the apostle. It would be wise for us to pray that the Lord would prevent Satan from retaliating against us when we exercise our authority against him in prayer.

Prayer realizes victory in spiritual warfare

God keeps us alert

Have you wondered why God allows such opposition to His people? One answer is that God uses demonic opposition to develop our character and discipline.

We become sensitive to the enemy's approach.

We need to be aware of when the enemy seeks to sneak up on us. We must not be caught unaware. Our military personnel in Pearl Harbor were taken by surprise and unable to respond when the Japanese attacked on December 7, 1941. Our fleet and sailors suffered devastating loss. Some ignored the report of strange aircraft approaching, and so they were horribly ruined by the enemy's bombers. We have clear warning from the Bible of the enemies and their tactics. We must be alert. "Be of sober spirit, be on the alert. Your adversary, the devil, prowls about like a roaring lion, seeking someone to devour" (1 Peter 5:8--9). Prayer keeps us in touch with the Lord and makes us sensitive to Satan's devices.

We learn to cast our concerns on God.

Satan can use our anxieties and our lack of confidence in God's sufficiency to provide and to protect. We must cast our cares on the Lord (1 Peter 5:6--7). We can keep from stumbling under attack. "Cast your burden upon the LORD, and He will sustain you; He will never allow the righteous to be shaken. But Thou, O God, wilt bring them down to the pit of destruction . . . But I will trust in Thee" (Ps. 55:22--23). When we see God answer our prayer and intervening on our behalf that will encourage us to continue to cast our concerns on Him. Psalm 120:1 declares, "In my trouble I cried to the LORD, and He answered me."

My wife and I counseled a tall young lady who used to play basketball but now could not, since she was suffering from what had been diagnosed as Fibromyalgia. We asked the Lord that if the enemy had anything to do with her malady, He would remove the disease. Her husband, my wife, and I not only prayed but commanded the enemy to leave her alone. Within one week, she was back playing basketball. The Lord had freed her from demonic interference! We all learned again to cast our concerns---even our infirmities---on the Lord.

God brings justice

Are you ever longing for justice? We can back off and turn our case over to God just as the Lord Jesus did (1 Peter 2:21--23). God is the ruler and judge. "Vengeance is mine, says the LORD" (Romans 12:19). He will care for us and requite our enemies as we obediently follow His leading.

There are many trials as our opponents attack.

Jesus predicted that in the world we would have trials. If the world hated Him, it would hate us. The servant is not above his master. We stand for Christ against unnumbered foes, and we and can expect opposition (John 15:18--19). Because of our union with Christ, He said, "You will have tribulation, but take courage. I have overcome the world" (John 16:33). We should not be surprised to face opposition. Many believers in lands dominated by false religions face persecution and deadly peril every day just because they are Christians. We can bring our battles before the Lord for His intervention for provision and protection.

Our Father and Judge will intervene as we persist in prayer.

Jesus told of a widow who constantly brought her need of legal protection before an unjust judge. The unsaved judge finally, reluctantly gave in to her repeated requests. The Lord drew the contrast: "Now shall not God bring about justice for His elect, who cry to Him day and night, and will He delay long over them? I tell you that He will bring about justice for them speedily" (Luke 18:7--8). The Lord Jesus told this parable "to show that at all times they ought to pray and not lose heart (Luke 18:1).

God delivers His own

He is our refuge and strength.

Do you feel unsafe and vulnerable in the battle? God is often pictured in the Psalms as a tower of strength and a fortress for His people. "God is our refuge and strength, a very present help in trouble. Therefore we will not fear . . ." (Ps. 46:1--2). "The LORD of hosts is with us; the God of Jacob is our stronghold" (Ps. 46:7).

We are safe in the arms of our Father. "He who dwells in the shelter of the Most High will abide in the shadow of the Almighty. I will say to the LORD, 'My refuge and my fortress, My God in whom I trust!'"
(Ps. 91:1--2).

He will answer when we call.

God says of those who are His and trust Him, "Because he has loved Me, therefore I will deliverer him. I will set him securely on high, because he has known My name. He will call upon Me, and I will answer him; I will be with him in trouble; I will rescue him and honor him" (Ps. 91:14--15). So we gain confidence as we realize that God actually intervenes and rescues us

Conclusion

What shall we then do in view of all of this? Let us put a high priority upon prayer for all things at all times. We must keep in fellowship and in contact with our Lord Jesus, the Captain of our Salvation and our Commander in the battle.

We must learn to pray regarding opposition and oppression. We cannot continue to be passive and ignore the reality of warfare and suppose that what we face is merely natural. Satan and his demons take advantage of our ignorance and humanistic approach to life. We must be aware of his tactics and beware of his devices. We must be on the alert. We must pray for discernment and deliverance in the battle.

We must stand in our position in Christ and exercise our delegated authority and become bold in spiritual warfare! If we don't, we shall certainly fail and fall prey to the enemy. If we do, we shall move on to victory after victory and enjoy the deliverance and freedom for which Christ died and rose again!

Questions to Ponder

1. What place does prayer play in spiritual warfare?

2. What authority do believers have to resist Satan and demons?

3. Do you know of examples of God's deliverance from spiritual enemies in the Bible or in human affairs?

4. In what ways does prayer contribute to victory in spiritual warfare?

CHAPTER 3

Spiritual Warfare Battle Tactics

God's tactics for Israel's overcoming enemy resistance varied. In the battle of Jericho, the army was directed to march around the heavily fortified city for seven days---once each day until the seventh when they marched around seven times. Then they blew their trumpets, and God caused the thick and towering walls to fall down and inward (Josh. 6).

With Gideon God reduced his forces to a ridiculous few---three hundred men. Then he used a surprise attack by night that confused and routed the Midianites (Jud. 7). To capture the city of Ai God directed Joshua to draw out the defenders by a staged retreat. And when the defending army came out to pursue an army of five thousand army hidden soldiers ambushed the enemy. So there was a great victory (Josh. 8).

In Israel's first battle Joshua met the enemy army head on. But Moses, Aaron, and Hur went to the top of a hill. As long as Moses lifted his staff in prayer and depended upon the power of God Israel prevailed. When he dropped his hands and staff the Amalekites prevailed. So Aaron and Hur held up Moses hands until Joshua overwhelmed Amalek (Ex. 17:8—16).

In each case God adopted the strategy the situation and taught His people the lesson of dependence upon Him for His wisdom and power.

Webster's Dictionary defines tactics as "the science and art of disposing and maneuvering troops or ships in action or in the presence of the enemy . . . Hence, any method of procedure; esp., adroit devices for accomplishing an end."

Tactics of warfare have varied and changed over history. But the tactics have been successful when there has been a unified plan and a competent director of the warfare. The highest level of planning is strategy. The intermediate level---the operational level---deals with the formation of units. Tactical decisions seek to obtain the greatest immediate value.

We have a wise and powerful commander in the Risen Lord Jesus. He has given us His plan in the Great Commission. We are to make disciples by going (reaching), baptizing (winning), and teaching (training) according to His Great Commission in Matthew 28:18-20. He has revealed features of His strategy in His Word. As we search and follow His Word we shall be able to win the battle for righteousness in the gospel. He has given us great promises and ordered us to pray that we might bear fruit for Him (John 14:12--15; 15:7--8).

Why do we need strategy and tactics in spiritual warfare praying? We must because we must take our stand in our position in Christ and exercise our privilege and power in the battle. Prayer is a basic weapon without which we cannot win the battle against evil.

Ephesians 6:10--18 was written against the background of pagan religions, the worship of demons, and the practice of demonically empowered magic. Consider the terms Paul used: "wrestle," "schemes," "principalities," "powers," "the devil." There is powerful and organized opposition to the gospel to the Savior, and to His servants.

In this unrelenting conflict Satan's forces are always on the offensive against the Church of Christ. They seek to deceive, divide, dominate, and destroy the forces of Christ. Many---if not most---Christians especially in Western society are unaware of the true dimensions of the battle with supernatural forces of evil. They are not aware of how it affects our personal and family lives, the local and international world scene, and our missionary personnel and program. Very few believers in Christ know about wrestling against such forces in warfare praying.

Let me encourage you and challenge you regarding our battle tactics in prayer. If we are to survive and succeed in the battle we must use effective tactics in warfare praying.

In warfare---us as in any good football, basketball, or soccer game---the team must have a good defense and a good offense. We need to pray in both defensive and offensive fashion to combat the demonic forces aligned against us.

One authority observes that defensive-offensive maneuvers include attack from a strong defensive position after enemy has been sapped of strength. The Lord Jesus has routed Satan and his demons by His death and resurrection and sits enthroned far above His enemies. And we are seated with Him in His victorious position (Eph. 1:19--2:6). We must adopt God-given and strategic tactics.

Our Prayer Defense

We are not without resources. God has given us prayer as communication with our commanding general. God has made wise provision for us. We can rely on Him wise arrangement for battle.

Defense by the Savior's Prayers

He has prayed for us.

The Lord Jesus prayed that God would keep us from being overwhelmed by the evil one (John 17:15). We shall never be taken over and removed from our relationship to the Lord. We are securely protected from eternal loss in the battle. Satan cannot dislodge us or keep us from the love of God (Rom 8:38-39). We need not fear the battle when He is by our side. We are on the winning side.

He is now praying for us.

The risen and exalted Savior is now in his humanity interceding for us at God's right hand as our High Priest. He took His office of Great High Priest upon His resurrection and ascension (Ps. 110: 1, 4; Heb. 10:12). He ever lives and keeps us in His grace. He will see us through to glory. He will help us and strengthen us along the way (Heb. 7:25; Rom 8:35--37).

Defense by the Saint's Prayers

As believer priests and saints we have authority to bring our requests before God in Christ's name. In this we must know something of the enemy's tactics to pray effectively.

Prayer for Prevention

We often are not aware of the subtle attacks of Satan. Our Western mind does not usually recognize his inroads and tactics. So we are caught off guard and surprised. We suffer intrusion and harm that could be prevented. Paul writes," With all prayer and petition pray at all times in the Spirit, and with this in view, be on the alert with all perseverance and petition for all the saints" (Eph. 6:18).

Protection from Evil. Our Lord directed us to pray for daily bread. He would also have us pray for daily protection from the evil one (Matt. 6:13). We can ask for the protection afforded by God's angels (Heb. 1:14). I don't think God wants unemployment in heaven.

When I was participating in a spiritual warfare conference in Pennsylvania I met a woman in the registration line who was dressed all in black. The next day as I was picking up my notes from a lecture on the occult, this same woman came down the church isle. She mounted three steps to the platform, for no one stopped her. I saw standing there with a nine-inch knife in her right hand. I whispered a prayer to the Lord and walked over to her. I said, "It's all right; give me the knife." She released the knife into my hand. I dropped it on the floor and gave her a hug. "It's OK; God loves you," I said. At that time some deacons escorted her away. The next day, I learned from one of the deacons that he had asked her what made her stop and wait at the edge of the platform. She told him that she came there to kill me, but she couldn't move any further. There were big angels standing in front of her to protect me. I had previously prayed---as I usually do---for protection. The Lord certainly answered that day!

A young man I had been counseling because of his problems stemming from Satanic ritual abuse was mowing my lawn. He had developed dissociative identity disorder (formerly called multiple personality disorder). One of his dissociative parts wanted to say something to me. I told him I would be glad to hear from that one called "Protector." This part said, "Dr. Dickason, do you know you have big angels around your house?" I answered, "I can believe that I do, but thank you for sharing that with me." Sometimes those who have been abused have unusual insight into the spirit world. God protects His own, so we can pray for our need protection from our enemies.

Unity among Believers. God desires unity of heart and mind among His people. That doesn't mean we always agree on everything, but it does means we are united on the basis of truth and love to honor Christ. Truth without love can be harsh. Love without truth can be misguided. Both are needed in true unity and harmony (Eph. 4:1--6).

A united front causes fear in our enemies (Phil. 1:27--28). When we present a united front, the opponents of Christ have a "sign of destruction for them." In suffering for Christ we can support one another. The cause of Christ must stand above individual preferences and concerns. This unity comes about through prayer and determination for mutual care. It is a testimony to a selfish and divided world. Christ prayed for our oneness (John 17:21) and established it by the baptism of the Holy Spirit at Pentecost (John 1:33; Acts 1:5; 2:1--4). We are now to maintain that established unity by our mutual care (Eph. 4:3--6). We need to ask the Lord to help us in this. The enemy would divide and conquer, as did the German army with their pincers movement in World War II.

We must forgive one another to avoid division in the church that Satan would cause (2 Cor. 2:6--11). Lack of forgiveness gives the devil a toehold---an opportunity to cause bitterness and rancor among the brethren (Eph. 4:26--27).

Church Health and Growth. God gave us an amazing immune system that wards off the enemies of our health and well being. We must pray for the health and well being of the Body of Christ, His Church. We should pray for the proper functioning of every part of the Body of Christ. This means respectful consideration and proper exercise of spiritual gifts in serving one another. This leads to unity, harmony, stability, spiritual development, and growth in quality and quantity of the membership (Eph. 4:12--16).

Christ recognized that the devil would oppose the building of His Church, but He plans and enables the success of His enterprise despite the forces of *hades*---the unseen spiritual world (Matt. 16:18). We pray against the evil spirits that oppose the Great Commission of reaching and building disciples for His Church. Satanists, witches, and New Age proponents pray against Christian enterprises and local churches on a regular basis--- particularly at the full moon and specified "holy days" throughout the year. We need to be aware of those days and pray for protection, health, and growth of the church.

The apostle Paul made requests along this line (Col.1:9--14). And we should recognize the great and sometimes horrible opposition to Christians world wide. There is particular persecution to Jews and Christians, because Satan hates those from whom the Messiah came and hates those who stand for the truth in Messiah Jesus. This is what Christ predicted would happen even at the hand of religionists (John 16:2, 33).

These are but a few matters of preventative prayer. Let us take our responsibility seriously, and let us raise a wall of defense against the aggressive attacks of the enemy!

Prayer for Relief

We often put up with unnecessary opposition and harassment from the devil. In those trying circumstances have you tried claiming your authority in Christ? Have you been praying specifically regarding the possibility of demonic intervention? Let me suggest several tactics we can use knowing what we do about spiritual warfare.

Praying against Harassment. Many have asked me about what to do about what seems to be spirits haunting their houses. The tactics are logical and simple if you know that warfare is real and if you understand some of the causes that might be involved. We can ask God to let us know what might have granted the spirits permission to stay in that area. The previous owners may have been involved in occult or demonic activity. There may have been some violence on the premises. There might be a curse on the property and the residents. God may give us some insights and acquaint us with the factual history. We can ask the Lord that if there have been such things---and He knows---that He would cancel the demonic claims and remove the harassing spirits and then dedicate the property to the Lord..

A psychiatrist and her husband---both believers in Christ---bought this corner property at a good price. I had helped her in counseling a client, so she knew of my experience. They invited me into their home, because she was experiencing a problem in her kitchen. Every time she neared the door going out to the garage the hair on her arms would stand on end. I asked about the condition of the house when they first entered. She said the west wall of the living room was painted black and that there was a raised platform. That seemed strange. I asked her if there was anything in the garage that was unusual. She said there was a heavy table that was on the platform. I suggested that the platform and the table might have been used in witchcraft ceremonies by the former residents. We asked the Lord that if that was the case to remove any curse or connection that allowed demons to claim permission to stay there. We dedicated the table to the Lord for His destruction, and they disposed of it. From that time on she had no eerie experience in the kitchen

A Christian builder had economic difficulties. He had built a beautiful house on a great corner property. After living in it for a time, he put it up for sale at a reasonable price. It didn't sell. He lowered the price twice, and it still didn't sell. Even other realtors were surprised. He called me, since the Lord had answered prayer to relieve another property problem. We prayed that the Lord would let us know what might be causing the problem this time. The Lord led him to find out that the woman across the street was a witch and was praying against the sale of his house. We prayed against her curses asking the Lord to break the power of the enemy working through her. His house sold shortly thereafter at a good price.

The same man had a similar with a new house just about completed. No one was interested in buying. He asked me to come to the house. I asked if he knew anything about the property on which it was being built. He said he found some American Indian artifacts in the side yard. Since Indians are involved in reverencing spirits that govern all of life, we asked the Lord to break the claim of any spirits to the property and dedicated it to the Lord Jesus. The house sold soon thereafter. We don't need to know the exact cause of the problem. We can always use the "if" question and commit the matter to the Lord.

Praying against Physical and Emotional Ailments. Not all ailments are caused by demons. Many are natural. However, with a biblical world view of the spirit world and their activities we would do well to commit the difficulties to the Lord for His solution. I and my wife, Jean (who is now with the Lord), counseled with college tall blond college student who loved to play basket ball but couldn't for five years due to her Fibromyalgia symptoms. She told us of some dark family problems. She gave us permission to check for the presence of demonic activity in her life. We found a spirit named "Infirmity" (as in Luke 13:11). We asked if he were causing or just aggravating the disease. She told us later that when we asked that question, she heard a discussion in her head, "Let's tell him we are just aggravating it." Her husband, who didn't believe this could happen to a Christian---as he was told by a missionary---had the privilege of asking the Lord to remove the Spirit of Infirmity and commanded him and any others out. The girl was back playing basketball within one week.

A pastor's wife in Colorado was afflicted with MS symptoms. The Lord relieved her of a demon also called Infirmity when her husband commanded him out. Another called 'The Magnificent One" who had given her supernatural discernment about others' mental and physical conditions---even at some distance---was also dismissed. She lost her so called "spiritual gift."

Demonization is often diagnosed by psychiatrists as either paranoid schizophrenia or bi-polar disorder, because some of the symptoms are similar---such as voices in the head, trouble with thought connections, or control by fears. We understand that there are natural diseases, but Satan is a great deceiver and a counterfeiter (2 Cor. 4:3--4; 11:14). Psychiatrists may be well trained from the natural standpoint and are of great help, but many are not aware of the intrusion of the spirit world into physical and mental areas. They are not trained by the secular and humanistic approach to test for demonic intervention. They are not acquainted with how to test or diagnose demonic influence. And if they were to do so, their licenses would be in danger from medical boards and the state. So many ignore this area, and many are fearful to investigate this reality. Christians informed and properly trained may be used by God to diagnose properly such cases. It is good to seek godly, experienced counsel.

Praying against Oppression. Many have been harassed by dark figures, by pressures on the body, by predictive dreams, or by intruding and repeated thoughts. Some have heard footsteps on staircases or walking through pianos. One of my counselees was told by a voice in her mind to drive off the bridge she was crossing. Another was told to drive into a telephone pole. Dr. Mark Bubeck reports that one woman was told to pick up a butcher knife and stab her child. In each case, there was a demon seeking to destroy the person. Satan is called a destroyer (*Abaddon* or *Apollyon*, Rev. 9:11) and a murderer (John 8:44). We need to shake off the restrictions of secular humanistic thinking and check out difficult situations by prayer.

Praying against Controlling Factors. When Satan declared, "I will make myself like the Most High" (Isa. 14:14) he wanted to be in control of everything. He lusted after the power and the glory that belonged only to the Eternal Creator God. So today he seeks to control our minds and bodies. He does this in many ways. He uses addictions, habits, debilitations. Humans are controlled by alcohol, drugs, and sexual desires. Drugs have been used to experience another realm of reality and to find a religious reality. Carolos Castaneda was taught by a Mexican medicineman how to transport himself into another world through the use of peyote beans. Heavy metal music with its emphasis on death and sex brings many into bondage. I have yet to meet a homosexual person who was not demonized and driven into his habits. I have found that the devil uses masturbation as a controlling sin that involves a fantasy forbidden by Christ (Matt. 5:27--30).

We need specific prayer to mount an adequate defense against Satan and his hosts for both prevention and relief of oppression.

Our Prayer Offense

The winning football franchise must have two capable teams---the defensive team and the offensive team. The defensive must stop the opponents from scoring. The offensive team must score the points to win. A balanced squad will get the best results.

To win the war we must not only set up defenses, but we must mount strategic attacks against the enemy. We can follow the example of the biblical prayers of godly kings and of the New Testament apostles. We can use the principles found in the imprecatory psalms that call for God's intervention.

Note David's prayer in our favorite Psalm 139.19. After praising God for His wonderful wisdom, power, and care, David prays against His enemies: "O that Thou wouldst slay the wicked, O God; depart from me, therefore, men of bloodshed." This is a godly man calling for God's judgment on the determinedly wicked. They are fixed in their opposition to God and to David, God's anointed king. When Jesus spoke of praying for our enemies He was speaking of personal enemies not God's enemies. In no way do we pray for blessing on demons. We need to realize that those who have taken their fixed stand against God and His people are displeasing to God. They hate God, and God must judge them. That may not seem to agree with the meek and mild picture some people see of the Lord Jesus. But He also spoke of His judgment on the wicked: "Depart from me, accursed ones, into the eternal fire which has been prepared for the devil and his angels" (Matt. 25:41). He is speaking of those who do not believe in the Messiah and have opposed His people. In 2 Thessalonians 1:7--8 Jesus is described as coming in flaming fire and "dealing out retribution to those who do not know God and to those who do not obey the gospel of our Lord Jesus." The Lord Jesus is not only the Savior; He is also the Judge. So imprecatory prayers are not out of order in our day.

Psalm 140 not only asks for rescue from violent men but also asks for God's proper retribution on evil, violent men: "As for the head of those who surround me, may the mischief of their lips cover them. May burning coals fall upon them; may they be cast into the fire . . . May evil hunt the violent man speedily" (Ps. 140:9--11). In praying this type of prayer, we must also ask that only the Lord's will be done. God is not obligated to hear improper prayers or prayers that do not fit His purposes.

Against Evil Influences in Governments

Daniel learned of demonic opposition to his prayer and to the angelic messenger sent to speak to him. The angel was delayed for three weeks because of the opposition of "the prince of the kingdom of Persia." Ephesians 6:12 would describe this one as a "world ruler"---a high ranking demon controlling the country and government of Persia. So fierce was the battle that Michael the archangel was sent to relieve the messenger angel so that the angel could deliver the message to Daniel. After the angel delivered the message to Daniel, he said, "But I shall now return to fight against the prince of Persia . . . and behold, the prince of Greece is about to come" (Dan. 10:13--20).

We can pray against governmental powers that are under demonic influence that God would limit their activity to oppose God's people and the spread of the gospel. Many missionaries experience difficulty of getting visas to a country. In countries dominated by other religions such as Hinduism, Buddhism, Islam, and Communism, there are direct oppositions, restrictions, persecutions, imprisonments, and executions of Christians. We should understand that these false religions are driven by demons.

Campus Crusade (CRU) reports that on one occasion when the team tried to show the Jesus film in India, they had trouble with projector and with the screen. The screen tore down the middle by itself. They learned that a Hindu witchdoctor was praying against the showing of the film. The CRU team prayed against the demonic opposition. The Lord intervened enabling them to show the Jesus film. We need to precede the presentation of the gospel and the sending of missionaries with fervent prayer against the enemy.

Consider the persistent problems in the Middle East. Communist and Islamic dominated countries violently oppose the gospel and persecute Christians. China, India, Sri Lanka, North Korea, and many countries of Africa are noted for their violent treatment of Christian converts and expatriates. Organizations such as Barnabas International, Voice of the Martyrs, and Slavic Gospel Mission report the needs of believers and suggest specific needed prayer.

We need to pray pointedly against the devil's work recognizing that we do not ultimately wrestle with human opposition but against Satan's well designed warfare against the Lord's truth and the Lord's people. We are to pray with "all prayer and petition at all times in the Spirit" (Eph. 6:18).

Against Evil Influences in Society

Rulers in Society

God saw to it that Daniel was strategically involved in government under several kings in the Persian area. He prayed three times each day. He was unashamed of his faith in the God of Israel and needed help in his responsible position. When he knew of the King Darius' edict that no one should pray to anyone other than the king he entered his house and prayed as usual with his windows open (Dan. 6:10). He was obviously praising the true God as well as praying for himself and his three friends whom God had previously delivered from the fiery furnace. He opposed the government edict.

The Apostle Paul urged us to pray "for kings and all who are in authority, in order that we may lead a tranquil and quiet life in all godliness and dignity" (1Tim. 2:2). Not all rulers promote godliness; rather some oppose it. We can pray against evil influences in our rulers and for God's influence in their responsibilities.

Secular Education

We have seen the banning of Christian influence, use of humanistic materials, ungodly administrators and teachers. They not only neglect a biblical world view but actively vey against it. Even to mention design in creation can result in dismissal from many college faculties. Even Christian institutions may promote evolutionist views of life and neglect the biblical view of creation. They may even refuse debate or discussion of other points of view. It may be that they are protecting their own academic reputation in the world's system. In the United States the Bible formerly was used as a reader. God could be mentioned and prayer practiced. Now these are banned as discriminatory. We need to pray for our administrators, teachers, and students that a balanced and fair approach to education might return to our schools. Too long have we suffered and allowed our children to be brainwashed by the influences of Darwin, Huxley, and John Dewey. Scientists of both secular and Christian persuasion have brought serious objections to the theory of evolution and of the materialistic origin of the universe. Evolutionists cannot account for the existence of Satan and demons. We can pray against evil influences and for godly influences in our educational systems. We can also become involved in the educational systems to stem the tide of antitheism and promote hearing again for proper spiritual emphasis.

Societal Health

Health System. There are threats to the health system. Socialized medicine may be a real problem. Delays and discrimination against the elderly and the "hopeless" by government decision can prevent needed care. The New Age holds that we are mini gods who control our destiny and our health. It is our responsibility to manage our own health and by extension the health of our society. Such ungodly control! We must pray against this influence and for the well-being of our people.

Moral Scene. With the refusal to recognize God and His moral laws we have liberty to choose our own way and life style. Following the imbalanced emphasis on women's liberation there came the uprising of gay and lesbian rights. These life styles are condemned by the Bible. They are a direct result of rejection of God the Creator and the substitution of idolatrous humanism and sexual perversion.

> For even though they knew God, they did not honor Him as God or give thanks . . . and exchanged the glory of the incorruptible God for an image in the form of corruptible man and of birds and four-footed animals and crawling creatures. Therefore God gave them over in the lusts of their hearts to impurity, that their bodies might be dishonored among them . . . For this reason God gave them over to degrading passions (Rom. 1:21--26).

We need to pray against the powerful and increasing influence of so called tolerance in moral matters (1 Cor. 5:1--2; 6:9--11). Perverted sex infects society and ruins humans made in the image of God.

We should pray against the practice of infanticide called abortion. Scientists tell us that there is no change in the essence of life from the first human cell to the development of a functioning human body. God allows procreation of a complete human being, body and spirit---a genuine human soul (Heb., *nephesh*) or being (Gen. 1:26; 5:1--3). In abortion, children are sacrificed for the convenience and pleasure of their parents. God who gives life expects us to protect and nourish that life. We sing, "Jesus loves the little children." That is true no matter what the age (Matt. 18:1--6). In ancient heathenism, adults sacrificed children to the gods for their protection and favor. Children were placed on the white hot arms of Baal or thrown into the hollow stomach of the idol to placate this false god. Today we rip children out of the womb for the convenience and betterment of adults. Our gracious God forgives those who repent of such evil, but there are lasting emotional and mental scars. We need to pray for those who have been through such a devastating experience. And we need to pray that many would be turned from such acts of child sacrifice so that children may live, develop, contribute to society, and have opportunity to trust Christ and live for Him. We can pray that abortion clinics would be shut down and that the law permitting abortions at any stage would be struck down.

Pornography along with human trafficking is the second largest industry in the world after illicit drugs. Idolatry always involves perverted sex. Ancient religions---such as the worship of Aphrodite or Diane or Astarte---all had prostitutes dedicated to the use of worshipers. Both female and male prostitutes served in this idolatrous way. The many breasted goddess of Hinduism exalts human sex and giving of life. We must pray against such perverted sex addiction and human trafficking. We can thank the Lord and pray for those groups that have taken up the challenge of ministering to those damaged by such practices. Pornography produces slavery to lust and ruins lives and marriages. Jesus spoke against fantasy as adultery in the heart (Matt. 5:27--28). We should pray that those involved would be convicted and turn from their evil ways.

False Religions. Humans were built to worship. If they don't worship the true and living God who created them, they will invent gods that they can worship. But we are creatures with great limitations. We are sinners with twisted minds and morality. The gods of our fashion are of human origination. They are either spirits that govern life to be feared and placated, or idols that represent spirits, or regulations determined to gain favor with gods of human concept. All the religions of the world have perverted sense of sex, except biblical Judaism and biblical Christianity, because they have the truth revelation from God in the Scriptures. All the religions of the world are legalistic and based on the principle that "good works" make us acceptable to God. Biblical Christianity holds that man is so engulfed in sin by his nature and his deeds that he cannot please God (Rom. 8:8).

Biblical Christianity holds that the Creator God rules in righteousness. He will save those who trust in His Son who became one of the human race to reveal God and to pay for our guilt of sin. God raised Him from the dead to prove that those who trust the Savior are forgiven and have right standing before God.

The Cults of Christianity present a Christ that either is less than God or not fully man. They minimize the guilt of sin before a holy God, and they assume that man can do something to ingratiate himself to God.

The other major religions of the world have another god or gods that Satan and his demons promote. All forms of idolatry are emboldened by evil spirits. Ancient religions of the Middle East sacrificed their children to demons by sacrificing them to idols (Ps. 106:34--38). The same was true of the human sacrifices made to the gods of the Incas and the Mayans of the Western Hemisphere. Satan operates in the realm of death all over the world and loves to be worshipped with blood sacrifices.

The practice of Satanism operates in America and Europe. It uses rituals that involve drinking blood and eating flesh to mock the Lord's Supper. It often involves human sacrifice. They consider that the younger and more innocent the sacrifice the more power they acquire.

Witchcraft (Wicca) involves the worship of a female goddess Diana and her male consort who takes the form of half-man and half-goat. Though they do not worship Satan directly both they and Satanism are worshipping demons. Their worship calendars are much the same. We can pray against their activities and curses they use when they meet on the morning of the day of the full moon.

The New Age gathers more adherents by many means. Eastern religious beliefs permeate the New Ages practices. Among these are psychic diagnosis, acupuncture, Reiki massage, reflexology, martial arts, and magical healings, and psychic diagnosis. A manager of a

New Age bookstore in North Carolina complained that she would have to close down because of the prayers of Christians in the area.

Secret societies involve seeking the real god through initiations and graduated instruction as to the true god. Spiritists seek information and insights from spirits of the dead who now have superior knowledge. Demons are happy to deceive and to accommodate these worshippers of false gods.

Against such influences we can pray to the risen and victorious Lord Jesus to discredit their teachings. to disable their power and to deliver those enslaved to them. We can pray that adherents would hear the gospel, that God would remove Satan's blinding (2 Cor. 4:3--4), that the Spirit of God would convict of sin (John 16:7--11), and that the Father would draw them to trust in the crucified and risen Savior (John 6:44).

Our Responsibility

With what we know about spiritual warfare from God's revelation and from what we know our culture and the prevailing world view of the world system we have a great responsibility to come before the true and living God and ask boldly that He would intervene specifically to defeat Satan's influence and activity in our present scene. We have slipped greatly from our biblical moorings and have welcomed false gods and world views to overtake our society.

We must face the on-going battle between the truth and the lie, between righteousness and godlessness, and between good and evil. God has given us the weapon of prayer. Let us claim our position in the crucified, risen and exalted Christ and exercise our delegated spiritual authority in prayer to the Creator and Judge. With urgent and dependent prayer we can open up opportunities for the spread of the gospel and growth of Christ's Church. We can defeat the enemy's schemes and activities. We cannot banish Satan from the earth or from all influence and control, but we can certain limit him significantly and specifically.

To win the ongoing spiritual war we must take advantage of specific prayer both for our defense and for our offense. We must recognize the reality of spiritual warfare. We must plan our tactics and work together in unity to encourage one another in the battle for truth.

Backed by Christ's universal and sovereign authority, aided by His intervention, strengthened by His provision, and encouraged by His promises, let us devote ourselves to serious and specific prayer to win the battle for the Savior.

Questions to Ponder

1. How can you pray specifically for defense against evil?

2. In what realms of society could we observe evil and pray against its manifestations?

3. How should we relate spiritual warfare to world religions and cults of Christianity?

4. What responsibility do we have in view of the intrusion of demonic propaganda and power in our personal lives or into our society?

CHAPTER 4

Spiritual Warfare Objectives

You will probably agree with nearly all parties in recognizing that the concentrated push in the Afghanistan war was a success even though the final outcome of the war lacked the shout of victory. The push was successful, because the objectives were clear and sufficient forces were aligned to accomplish the goal.

In any war, soldiers must know what they are seeking to accomplish and what strongholds there are to be taken on the way to achieving victory. Our ultimate goal is to honor the Lord Jesus Christ and to build His church. But what are some of the immediate objectives we need to take in seeking to win the war against our enemies---Satan and his armies of demons?

Our spiritual warfare is not ultimately against flesh and blood but against demonic forces active in many areas of the world scene and in our personal lives. Prayer is the concentrated fire power that prepares the way for invading the enemy's territory and completing the battle plan of freeing people from His bondage so that they might enjoy God and the life He has designed for them. In preparation for the landing of the troops of WW II on the beaches of France, Allied ships bombarded the coast fortifications with specific heavy shelling. We must bombard the enemy forces with our prayers that are powerful in Christ for the pulling down of strongholds of Satan (2 Cor. 10:3--4).

To take our objectives in spiritual warfare we must concentrate our fire power by prayer on specific targets. What are some specific objectives that we should seek to take in concentrated prayer? Let me share with you three specific biblical objectives---immediate goals---in warfare praying. These may give you further insight into applying this type of praying.

Winning Persons to Christ

The risen Lord Jesus gave us His Great Commission to make disciples of all nations. This is to be done by going or reaching the lost, by baptizing or winning and enlisting believers, and by teaching them all that He commanded (Matt. 28:18--20). This is our assignment from our Commander in Chief. We must recognize that there are great problems that must be met by specific and concentrated prayer.

Problems to Overcome

The problems we face in winning persons to Christ are insurmountable by human wisdom and schemes. We cannot depend solely on human programs, power, and efforts. The obstacles require God's powerful intervention for removal. What are some of those obstacles?

Ignorance of the True Gospel

So many people have never really understood the gospel. Many times the sharing or preaching of what is supposed to be the gospel is incomplete, garbled, or twisted. How shall anyone truly believe the truth and receive Christ without clear and simple presentation of the gospel? The gospel must be clearly delivered and clearly understood to be received.

A proper presentation of the gospel should include the following: (1) we are guilty of sin, (2) Christ died as our substitute to make a complete payment of our debt of sin and rose again from the dead, and (3) we must simply trust Christ as our personal Savior.

With some we must first establish that God is the creator and judge who is holy and righteous. He demands sinners to pay their sin debt or have sufficient substitute pay it for them. Christ is that sufficient substitute. His once-for-all death is a complete payment to God for all sins (Heb. 9:12, 26). God fully and finally forgives those who do nothing but trust Christ, His Son and Savior. Where there is forgiveness of all sin, there is no more sacrifice or further payment needed or accepted (Heb. 10:14--18). The Lord Jesus cried on the cross, "It is finished!" not "it is begun" (John 19:30). We must share this pointedly with people that they might understand and genuinely trust the Savior who took the judgment for our guilt fully once for all (Heb. 9:12).

Natural Blindness to the Gospel

The natural man---the one who has never been born again and has never received the Holy Spirit upon receiving Christ---is unable to comprehend and welcome the truth of the gospel. It even seems moronic or nonsensical to him (1Cor. 2:14). He does not have the capacity to welcome the truth in Christ. This is natural blindness of the man left only to his own discernment. It is only through the Spirit of God that a person can be enlightened to the truth in Christ.

Satanic Blinding to the Gospel

If the gospel is hidden from a person's understanding, it is not only natural blindness but Satanic or demonic blindness that prevents understanding that the gospel is true. As the apostle Paul said, "If our gospel is veiled, it is veiled to those who are perishing, in whose case the god of this world has blinded the minds of the unbelieving, that they might not see the light of he gospel of the glory of God in Christ, who is the image of God" (2 Cor. 4:3--4). Satan is determined to prevent the spread and reception of the truth so that persons would not be saved. We are in spiritual battle for the minds of mankind!

These are great and formidable barriers. We cannot overcome them by relying on our programs, our persuasion, and our power. We are driven to depend upon our God!

Prayer that Overcomes

If we are insufficient and helpless in this battle to present the gospel, then we must turn in complete dependence upon the living and almighty God, our strength and our sufficiency (2 Cor. 3:5). The Bible instructs us as to what we should pray for communication of the gospel and enlightenment about Christ and Salvation.

Communication of the Gospel

Messengers. We must pray for the proper presentation of the gospel. How can anyone respond to the gospel if they don't hear it? As Romans 10:14 says, "How shall they call upon Him in whom they have not believed? And how shall they believer in Him whom they have not heard? And how shall they hear without a preacher?" We should pray that God would send messengers to share the gospel.

Circumstances. God can arrange the methods and conditions necessary for the proclamation of the gospel. We can pray for freedom to present and openness to receive the gospel. He can open doors and break down barriers to sharing the gospel. We can pray that qualified believers would contact our unbelieving friends with the gospel. God can bring into theirs lives His servants who can befriend them and share the truth of salvation in Christ. We can pray that the Lord of the Harvest would send harvesters (Matt. 9:37).

Enlightenment to the Gospel

Removal of Satanic Blinding. Only God can remove the veil that the powerful fallen angel Satan uses to keep unbelievers from seeing the bright and glorious truth in Christ. We can pray for the removing of this blinding, since we have authority in Christ to ask for such a supernatural enlightenment. God commissioned Paul with gospel that can "open their eyes so that they may turn from darkness to light and from the dominion of Satan to God, in order that they may receive forgiveness of sins" (Acts 26:18).

Conviction by the Holy Spirit. The Holy Spirit supplies a necessary step in moving an unbeliever to trusting Christ. The Lord Jesus spoke about great opposition to the gospel and His messengers. How were they to communicate the gospel in the face of such resistance? The disciples were to witness to Him and the Holy Spirit would also witness with them (John 15:26--17). He would empower them. They would preach, but Holy Spirit would make the gospel clear and real to unbelievers. The Lord said it was necessary that He go to the Father so He could send the Spirit to do the necessary work of conviction of the unbelieving world. What does that involve?

Conviction is more than making the gospel plain; it involves convincing the person of the truth of the gospel and that it applies to him. It is bringing the gospel home to the heart of the individual. The Holy Spirit essentially says, "This good news is for you! You must receive Christ or face judgment."

But what is the content of this conviction by the Spirit? Jesus makes it clear. First, it involves clarification of the *guilt of sin*, because the unbeliever has not trusted Christ for the forgiveness of his sin Second, it involves the realization of *God's righteousness*; because the Savior has been proved to be righteous in that God raised Him from the dead, exalted Him, and gives righteousness to those who trust Him. Third, it includes the warning of *judgment;* because the greatest of all sinners, Satan, has been judged by the cross and that God will judge all those involved in his evil worldly kingdom.

That means that the sharing of the gospel message should include these three truths so that the Spirit may use them to bring the sinner to recognize that he must respond positively to the gospel or face God's judgment.

Drawing by the Father. Jesus said that no one is able to come to Him except the Father draws that person (John 6:44). The Father calls sinners to come to Christ and moves in their hearts to trust in the Savior. Without the Father's causing sinners to come to Christ no one can be saved. So we must pray for the Father's gracious drawing the individual to faith in Christ.

Building Persons in Christ

The Lord Jesus desires and designs the building of His Church (Matt. 16:18). This involves adding people to His Body and building members of His Body in spiritual maturity.

There are at least 16 New Testament passages that picture genuine believers engaged in spiritual warfare with Satan and his armies. From these and related passages we can learn how to pray for the building up of believers.

Standing in Assurance

The enemy plants doubt and undermines our growth (Col. 2:2). He knows that if he can undermine our confidence in our salvation and relationship to Christ, he has us at a great disadvantage. In doubt and fear we have lost our ability to stand with confidence in our safety and authority in Christ. We need to be strengthened and stand in the power and authority that we have in the risen and victorious Savior against all the devil's schemes (Eph. 6:10--11).

We are secure in God's salvation. The Father and His Son guard us and keep us from the evil one. This is the prayer of the Lord Jesus: "Father, I desire that they also, whom Thou hast given me, be with Me where I am, in order that they may behold My glory . . ." (John 17:24). We are safe in the hands of both the Son and the Father (John 10:28--30). The accuser of the brethren seeks to cause us doubts and fears about our acceptance with God (Rev. 12:10). His fiery arrows are designed to confuse us and upset our trust in God. We must raise the shield of confidence in God and His Word to ward them off. We can pray not only for ourselves but for those who battle those doubts and fears that they would recognize from where these disturbing thoughts come and stand firm in the grace and power of Christ.

Protection from False Doctrine and Life Style

The enemy promotes all sorts of distractions and deterrents to spiritual growth and effective service for Christ. The enemy distorts the biblical truth about Christ and His salvation. Other errors include such things as legalism, mysticism, asceticism, and perfectionism. We need to guard ourselves from these hindrances to fellowship and development of the spiritual life. We can pray against these influences in the lives of believers (1Tim. 4:1--2, 6; Col. 2:15—3:4).

False Teachings

False teaching may deny His full deity as the eternal Son of God, virgin birth, unique miracles, resurrection from the dead, ascension and coming again. He is genuine deity and genuine humanity without sin united in one eternal person forever. Salvation has been accomplished by Christ's full payment for our sins on the cross (Heb. 10:10--18). What is the condition for receiving salvation? We must by faith alone trust Him alone to forgive our sins and grant us right standing before God. Any addition to these terms will cause us to loose confidence in our standing before God and our authority to face Satan (Eph. 2:7--8).

Legalism

Legalism is an attitude of seeking self-advancement by following a set of rules---an attempt to gain favor with God or man through a code of conduct. This engenders pride and improper self-confidence, promotes a critical attitude toward oneself and others, and divides believers into achievers and non-achievers. In this error, we are always comparing ourselves with others and promoting selfish competition. It separates the believer from the grace of God as the source of daily productive living for Christ. We can pray that believers would recognize their perfect acceptance with God, rely upon the Holy Spirit, and respond with a life of love of God and others (Gal. 5:1--12, 14--15, 18).

License

This is a practice of living without restrictions satisfying one's own desires (Gal. 5:13). It manifests the works of the flesh (Gal. 5:16--21). License rejects the control of the Holy Spirit and chooses to exercise control by the flesh. This results in loss of fellowship with Christ, interferes with ability to serve Christ and others, and invites the chastisement of God. We can pray that those living for their own desires would see it as rebellion against a loving God, that they would submit to God, and allow the Spirit to cultivate their lives (1 John 1:9; Rom. 12:1--2).

Mysticism

Mystics believe that truth may be known by direct personal insight or spiritual sense, often apart from reasonable use of the mind or regulation by Scripture. They claim to have a special insight to God and His will. They will often urge other to seek the same experience. This is related to magical or occultic practice. The danger with mysticism is that is limits the secret truth to the insiders. This is often seen in secret societies or in charismatic groups. It appeals to supernatural experiences and opens the door to demonic influences. We can pray for those involved that they would (1) recognize God's universal truth revealed in Christ and the Bible (Col. 1:15--20), (2) rest in Christ as the totality of God's wisdom and power (Col. 2:1--7), (3) refuse false claims to secret truth and power (Col. 2:8; 16--19), and (4) refocus their minds on Christ and their union with Him (Col. 3:1--15, 16).

Perfectionism

In ethics this is the doctrine that perfection of moral character or man's ideal nature is the supreme ethical end of man. It denies what the Bible teaches about human depravity and sin and seeks to establish one's own moral achievements. In practice, the perfectionist insists that all must be done perfectly or there will be hurtful consequences. This leads to self-centered motives and efforts. It promotes pride and drivenness and contributes to a legalistic outlook and criticism of others. Perfectionism disappoints and discourages and leads to self-condemnation and even suicidal tendencies. It fails to recognize the value of life and the worth of others. Deliverance is found in recognizing that this error hinders growth and development, confessing it, rejecting it, and claiming back occasion given to the devil. We can pray that those trapped would confess their pride and self-sufficiency and that they would submit to the Holy Spirit for His cultivation.

Occult Involvement

Occult practices seek secret wisdom and secret power. The occult involves divination or fortune telling, magic, and spiritism (channeling), and various combinations. It is strictly forbidden by God (Deut. 18:9--13). There are many popular forms. These involve witchcraft, magical healing, psychic diagnosis, charms, astrology, acupuncture and acupressure, martial arts, holistic healing, New Age meditation, Yoga, and such things. We can pray that those involved in such things would recognize that they are contrary to the Word of God, repent, and turn back to Christ, His truth, and His healing. They need to trust Christ for their needs and cultivate a biblical life style.

In each of the above errors, one must (1) confess the sin, (2) cancel the ground given to the devil and (3) command the demonic forces to desist and depart to where the Lord Jesus sends them. We can pray they would rest in Christ for His gracious perfect acceptance, obey Him, and adopt a humble and thankful heart for God's grace.

Good Personal Relationships

God made us in His image as social beings. He promotes all good personal relationships. Satan hates what God has created and designed. He attacks all good personal relationships. He substitutes and promotes his own design for destruction.

The enemy attacks the family and marriages.

Right from the beginning Satan interfered with the marriage relationship. He tempted Eve to disobey the authority of Adam, leading her to eat the forbidden fruit. Satan then moved Adam to obey Eve to eat of the fruit also. Rules and roles were ignored. Both husband and wife suffered the consequences of sin, and so did the whole human race. We still have trouble with order in the household, so that the apostle Paul had to remind us that wives are to submit to their husbands and that husbands are to love their wives as Christ loved the church and gave himself for her. Husbands should administrate their households in godly fashion (Eph. 5:22--33; 1 Tim. 3:4--5). Remember the Ephesians and other peoples lived in a society highly influenced by fear and obedience to wicked spirits.

Satan seeks to break up marriages and families. He promotes disobedience. He promotes separation and divorce and causes unfaithfulness in the marriage covenant. Paul warns Christians against improper sexual relationships. He says that it not necessary as it was in pagan societies and religions to have sexual intercourse outside of marriage. Yet to avoid such, he urged those to marry who could not stay single. He urged married couples to have regular sexual relationships "lest Satan tempt you because of your lack of self-control" (1 Cor. 7:5). Sexual union is designed to find fulfillment in God ordained marriage. Fornication and adultery will incur God's judgment (Heb. 13:3).

We must pray for godly marriages, for good relationships between partners, for godly management of the home, for godly example to the children, and against Satan's influence and control.

The enemy divides the family of God.

When Paul urged the Corinthians to discipline the man who was living with his father's other wife (1 Cor. 5:1--5) they excommunicated him. When he repented and broke off that ungodly relationship, the apostle urged the church to forgive and receive him back to fellowship "in order that no advantage be taken of us by Satan; for we are not ignorant of his schemes" (2 Cor. 2:11--12). Satan would divide and conquer. We are to forgive and restore not differ and divide.

During WW II the Nazis used the "pincers movement" to effectively fight Allied forces. Heavily armored divisions drove through the Allied lines at two separated points. They swiftly moved to close behind the lines to surround their opponents to divide and then conquer when the main army moved up. Satan uses similar tactics. When Paul said "we are not ignorant of his schemes," he was not speaking of Christians in general. Most Christians are unaware to Satan's tactics, because they have not studied what the Bible reveals about spiritual warfare. He spoke from the vantage point of what he and his companions knew about the enemy's methods of attack.

We need to be aware of the devil's schemes and pray against them. We can pray for unity and loving communication. We can also pray for and practice proper discipline in the church. In this we need to pray for church leadership to be bold to exercise responsibility.

Deliverance from Discouragement and Defection

If Satan can undermine our confident stand in the love, power, and grace of God, he can work havoc in our lives individually and corporately.

Satan attacks our confidence and our hope.

If Satan and his helpers can undermine our confidence in God and His Word, he has gained a great advantage. We have lost our sure footing and will slip. This is the reason why we need the shield of faith as part of the armor of God (Eph. 6:17). The fiery darts demons send are designed to cause fear and distract us from our confidence in the Lord's protection and sufficiency. We must declare our trust in God's goodness, truth, love, and wisdom. We can pray that we and our fellow believer-warriors may stand firm and raise that shield of confidence in God and His Word. It is forever settled in heaven (Ps. 119:89). It needs to be settled in our hearts.

Satan seeks to thwart our plans and service.

The apostle said that he tried more than once to come to the Thessalonians, but Satan hindered him from doing so. "Satan thwarted us" (1 Thess. 2:18). Satan hinders believers at times from what we would like to do for Christ and His people. If he can hinder the apostle, he can hinder us too. Paul was also concerned that the tempter might have led some away from the faith (1 Thess. 3:5, 10).

Even though the Lord allows such things we would do well to pray against the enemy's plans to disrupt good plans to share the Word and build the church.

Relief from Oppression

We often forget that we wrestle not only against human opposition but against spiritual forces in the heavenlies. Demons can directly and personally oppress believers in mind and body as with a "thorn in the flesh"(2 Cor. 12:7) or use humans to oppose believers (2 Thess. 3:1—2).

Satan moves human authorities against believers.

The Lord Jesus warned the church of Smyrna that the devil is about to cast some of them into prison and that they would have tribulation. He urged them, "Be faithful until death, and I will give you the crown of life (Rev. 2:10). Recently we have witnessed radical groups in Africa, India, Nepal, Sri Lanka, and CIS countries severely beat, imprison, and kill believers in Christ for their faith. Believers in the groups' estimations are threats to and opponents of their society's values and goals.

Saints need to pray about human authorities.

The Spirit of God through the apostle Paul urged us to pray for those in authority that we might lead a godly and peaceable life. Our leaders are appointed or allowed by God to be in power (Rom. 13:1--7). We need to pray for our country and for our leaders that might fulfill properly the role assigned them by God. We can pray for wisdom and correct attitudes and actions that will benefit all the people---especially Christians (1 Tim. 3:1--8). We can pray that actions of wicked authorities be stopped and that God would change their minds and the circumstances.

Deliverance from Temptation

Matthew records that Satan is "the tempter" who opposed Christ in the wilderness (Matt. 4:1--3). Tempting to sin is one of Satan's best schemes to distract and disable Christians.

Satan uses affliction to oppose our stand in Truth.

False teaching about the Rapture had greatly shaken the Thessalonians. It came through a spirit or a spoken word or a forged letter to the effect that they were already in the Tribulation Period. Paul had taught that the tribulation would follow the Rapture of the Church (2 Thess. 2:1, 5). Most likely demonic deception was involved, no matter what the means---a spirit, a message, or a letter. This resulted in great mental and emotional distress in the congregation, because the apostle had assured them that they would not go through the Tribulation. The timing was the issue not courage. Paul mentions the deception that Satan will cause in the Tribulation by using false miraculous type of powers or magic (2 Thess. 2:9). The Lord Jesus told the church in Smyrna that Satan's people would cast some of them into prison (Rev. 2:8--11).

All throughout church history Christians have been persecuted and martyred due to demonic opposition and often by false religions. And so it is today. Some estimate that there have been more martyrs in the last fifty years than through all the preceding centuries since Christ. We must pray for those so persecuted says the New Testament (Heb.13:3).

Christ wants us to pray daily against the enemy's tactics.

In the Lord's pattern prayer, He gives us major matters about which to pray. Included is prayer for our daily bread---our physical needs. We must also pray for daily protection from the evil one---a point that is often overlooked by those lacking a biblical view of the spirit world. We are to pray that we not be led into such temptation that would allow Satan to overcome us (Matt. 6:9--17).

Freeing Persons from Demonic Bondage

Reasons for Bondage

I suggest the acronym APT for the ways in which demons may intrude into our lives. That stands for ancestral sins, personal involvement in things occult or demonic, and transfer from attempted control of mind or body by someone demonically controlled.

Ancestral Sins

The Second Commandment forbids the worship of false gods. God blesses those who obey the true God and worship Him only, but God promises judgment upon those who indulge in worship of false gods and the associated lifestyle even down to the third and fourth generations of the family line (Ex. 20:4--6). This judgment or curse scrolls down the generations until a person confesses and cancels the sins of past generations just as did Daniel (Dan. 9:4-12-16) and Nehemiah (Neh. 1:6; 9:32--37). Some say that Ezekiel 18:1-4 cancels that curse; but both Daniel and Nehemiah lived after Ezekiel. Further Jesus and Paul spoke of their present generation experiencing God's judgment for sins of their ancestors (Matt. 23:32--36; Luke 11:47--50; Rom. 1:21--32; 5:12--21). Note also that Ezekiel refers not to the Second Commandment but to a current proverb the people were using to excuse their own sin. The curse of the Second Commandment continues.

This is true today. More than 95% of the over 650 persons I have counseled in the last forty-six years have experienced demonic opposition stemming from their ancestral past. False religion, violence, sexual deviation, suicide, involvement in secret organizations, etc. must be confessed and renounced before the God of our Lord Jesus Christ to obtain freedom and healing from demonic harassment. Many physical and mental maladies have been relieved by specific prayer in the authority of Christ. Whether the ancestral past sins are known or not the wise and godly approach should be to confess the sin, cancel the ground, and command the enemies to release their hold and to depart to where Christ sends them.

A pastor's wife in Colorado suffered the symptoms of multiple sclerosis. She shared that she had special insight into peoples' personal difficulties---physical or mental. She said her parents had the same "gift from God." I counseled her along with her husband regarding the fact that no one can by normal or godly means know another's thoughts (1 Cor. 2:11). This was an ancestral occult power. She with her husband confessed and renounced this power and practice. We found that a spirit who called himself "The Illustrious One" was giving her occult powers. The Lord dismissed him when they command him in Jesus' authority to go. We found another demon by the name of "Infirmity" who confessed he had caused her frequent symptoms of MS. His name was the same as the one Jesus dismissed from the woman in Luke 13:10--13---"spirit of infirmity." This Christian couple also commanded this one to leave in Jesus' name, and she was relieved of the MS symptoms. However the district superintendent of the denomination did not agree with such measures; and his opposition led them to leave to serve in another group in another state.

Not all physical or mental problems are caused by demons, but it is a wise thing to check out the issue by proper testing to see if demons are involved.

Personal Sins

Personal sins may allow demonic oppression or even invasion. (See my book, *Demon Possession and the Christian*, available at

Amazon). We must pray specifically about these with confession and renunciation and then command the spirits to leave in the authority delegated to us by Christ. These sins may involve occult practices of divination, magic, or attempted contact with spirits. Other sins give the enemy opportunity, such as rebellion in any form, pride and self-promotion, bitterness and grudges, lack of forgiveness, sexual misconduct or perversion, pornography, masturbation, improper use of drugs or alcohol, involvement in martial arts, New Age meditation or other practices, involvement in false religions or cults, and seeking questionable healing or special spiritual gifts. We can deal with these for ourselves or help others in seeking the Lord's deliverance from demonic powers. God is faithful to forgive and cleanse (1 John 1:9). If we submit to God, He will free us (Jas. 4:7).

Transferred influences

Another avenue of demonic oppression comes from improper treatment received, especially from those occultly or demonically involved. If someone has been hypnotized, had an astrology chart cast, visited a fortune teller, had hands laid on to be healed or to speak in tongues, been diagnosed by magical or new age practitioners, been physically or sexually abused, there is likelihood of demonic transference. Such experiences should be confessed, renounced, and demons commanded to leave in Christ's name.

Some good Christian people or teachers may not agree with the above suggestions, but they have not the biblical backing or the clinical experience to challenge successfully these suggested treatments for spiritual freedom and healing. They must have clear contrary biblical teaching and be able to evaluate and disprove first hand the experiences of many godly and biblically grounded counselors who have had many years of successful practice. No one can prove that Christians have never been invaded, for no one can prove a universal negative. That would require detailed investigation of all Christians of all eras of history or a direct, substantiated, non-controversial statement of Scripture directly to that effect. (Again check out my investigative book, *Demon Possession and the Christian* at Amazon.)

Relief from Bondage

Let me list briefly steps that can be taken to find relief from demonic opposition and bondage.

Too many believers are ignorant of the details of spiritual warfare and fearful to take their stand in opposition to Satan and his demons. We need to take our stand in the authority of the risen and conquering Savior and carry the battle to the enemy! Here are some practical suggestions.

1. Renounce demonic causes and powers (Acts 8:22--24).
2. Confess occult and controlling sins (Acts 19:18--20).
3. Dedicate your life to Christ for His control (James 4:7; Rom. 12:1--2).
4. Cancel any ground (opportunity) given to Satan (James 4:7).
5. Break any curses or spells against you or your family (Matt. 6:13).
6. Sever improper relationships (Eph. 5:11--12).
7. Destroy occult objects (Acts. 19:18--20).
8. Ask God to break any satanic schemes and conspiracies against you (Matt. 6:13).
9. Pray against human agents controlled by demons (2Thess. 3:1--2).

Conclusion

Christ Jesus came to destroy the works of the devil (I John 3:8). By His cross Christ ruined the power of Satan and demons (Heb. 2:14--15; John 12:31; Col.2:15). We can take our stand in

Christ's victory accomplished by His death and resurrection. We can press for the application of that victory in our personal lives, in our families, in our church, and in our society.

Note God's promise to Joshua (Josh. 1:2--3, 5).

> Moses, My servant is dead; now therefore arise, cross this Jordan, you and all this people, to the land which I am giving to them, to the sons of Israel. Every place on which the sole of your foot treads, I have given it to you, just as I spoke to Moses . . . No man will be *able* to stand before you all the days of your life. Just as I have been with Moses, I will be with you; I will not fail you or forsake you.

See how God's promise came true (Josh. 21:43--45; 23:3).

> So the LORD gave Israel all the land which He had sworn to give to their fathers, and they possessed it and lived in it . . . Not one of the good promises which the LORD had made to the house of Israel failed; all came to pass. And you have seen all that the LORD your God has done to all these nations because of you, for the LORD your God is He who has been fighting for you.

There were pockets of resistance because of incomplete trust and obedience (Josh 2:23). These became thorns in their sides and prevented enjoyment of Israel's inheritance. We also have the promise, "I will never desert you, nor will I ever forsake you." (Heb. 13:5). We must press on toward complete victory.

We need to develop big feet of faith and to walk in obedience. Then we can by praying for specific objectives win our spiritual warfare by prayer to the only true and living God who sent His Son to destroy the works of the devil (1 John 3:8).

Questions to Ponder

1. In view of spiritual opposition, how may we specifically pray that persons would come to Christ?

2. What obstacles should we pray against in promoting building of individual believers and of the church?

3. How does what you are learning affect the way you pray for your missionaries and pastors?

4. Have you noted some instances where you suspect demonic influences against which you can pray?

5. What methods of approach to our minds do demons use to bring oppression? How can you pray about these?

CHAPTER 5

Practical Pointers in Spiritual Warfare

A combat soldier receives training and conditioning that readies him to face the demands, dangers, and opportunities found in the field of battle. The soldier's equipment must be ready. In the days of musket loaders, the cry was, "Keep your powder dry!" Today, a foot-solder must keep his automatic rifle clean, oiled, and ready to function. He is trained to take his gun apart and reassemble it while blindfolded.

Our spiritual weaponry must be kept in good condition and in constant readiness. The soldier's attitude must be alertness. The soldier in the field is taught to "sleep with one eye open." He is conditioned to wake at the slightest strange noise or movement. He cautiously awakes to assess the situation, and grasping his weapon kept close at hand he moves to defend or attack decisively.

Many Christians have not kept their spiritual weaponry in good working order and close by.

Many have been caught napping and not ready for Satan's sly and sudden attack. The apostle Peter warns believers, "Be of sober spirit; be on the alert. Your adversary, the devil, prowls about like a roaring lion, seeking someone to devour" (1 Peter 5:8).

If we are to pray effectively and be victorious in spiritual warfare, there are certain practical matters of preparedness and perspective we must maintain.

What are some of these practical matters that contribute to victory and aid us in spiritual warfare praying? Let me suggest several.

Preparedness for the Battle

Note the text of 1 Peter 5:8: "Be to be of sober spirit." We must be self-controlled, not lax in discipline, not distracted by non-essentials, keeping our minds on our main goals for the Lord. In the context that means realize the reality of the battle.

Note first, "Be on the alert." This requires us to be vigilant, check out the pitfalls, dangers, and to be sensitive to the enemy's schemes and pressures.

What is the danger? We must face "your adversary." He is Satan who opposes our good and seeks our harm. Who is he? "The devil"---the one who would slander us! The Greek *diabolos* pictures our enemy as one who trips us up as one who throws a trip stick between the legs of a runner..

What is his activity? He "prowls about like a roaring lion." He is a strong and deadly foe stealthily moving in for the kill. A missionary kid from South Africa, said his father could not understand why Satan was called a roaring lion on the prowl, because lions were quietly stalking their prey. They roared only afterward the kill to tell of their victory and warn others to stay away. I would suggest that Peter describes Satan as a notoriously successful hunter who now sneaks about quietly to target his next victim.

What is Satan's objective? He is "seeking someone to devour." He would sink his teeth into you, chew you up into little pieces, and swallow you down. This is the meaning of the Peter's Greek word for devour.

What specific matters of preparedness must we consider that we might be successful in battle?

Alertness

Readiness Rather Than Over Reaction

When we run into difficulty we must have our hearts ready and armor on. We must have preparation without panic. Remember God is in control. We are able to resist in His strength (Eph. 6:10).

Sensitivity Rather Than Superstition

We need to be open to the reality of demon opposition and to the possibility of specific attacks. We can pray, "Lord, if the enemy has his hand in this, make us aware of what we need to know and please relieve us of his attacks." We don't need to see a demon behind every bush, but we do need to recognize bushes. Demons love to hide behind unsuspected occasions or persons. Duck hunters hide behind blinds while they sound their inviting duck calls. So the enemy has decoys and devices to attract us. We must be sensitive to his schemes and devices.

Openness Without Over Attributing

Beware of the superstitious approach that borders on fear or uses magical means to ward off the enemy. I know of some Christian counselors who anoint door knobs and windows to keep out demons. It is superstitious and naïve to think that demons are intimidated and prevented from intruding by such magical means. Only dependent prayer in the authority of Christ is effective. Some would use the sign of the cross or holy water to restrict demons. I think that demons laugh at such ineffective, superstitious means. It is application of the authority of the risen and victorious Christ that prevents and opposes demonic activities.

The International Center for Biblical Counseling (predecessor of Deeper Walk International) was about to hold a spiritual warfare conference in Sioux City, Iowa. Some of us who were presenters walked around the convention center praying that the Lord would protect the grounds and the attendees and that He would keep the evil one from interfering. The bankers of western Iowa meeting there at the same time had arranged a psychic for entertainment. When she sought to perform her spiritistic, magical arts she was very frustrated. She could not perform as usual. We found out later that she finally gave up, and we gave thanks to the Lord for His intervention.

Allegiance

As in any warfare we must obey our commanders. Neglect of duty invites discipline. Desertion is reprehensible and has repercussions. We must follow closely the orders we receive and not deviate; or we will face isolation, lack of support, and defeat. The Christian warrior must be subject to Christ and be determined to follow orders.

Submission

James 4:7 gives the formula for successful procedure in our war with Satan and his armies. We are to submit to God. This is the primary requirement. Without this step, we cannot expect victory. We must submit our own persons---all of our life---to our Commander in Chief, our victorious and exalted Savior, the Head of the Church. We must be determined to follow Christ. We must present our minds and our bodies to Christ as Lord (Rom. 12:1--2). The members of our body should become instruments of righteous warfare to God in standing against sin and Satan (Rom. 6:13).

It is our duty to present our children to the Lord in meaningful dedication to the Lord for His development and protection from the evil one. All life belongs to God, and we recognize that when we dedicate our children to Him. We must not think that the enemy would not touch them; but we need to keep watch over them, for they belong to the Lord.

I counseled a missionary child whose parents were graduates of a Bible college. They served in Pakistan. They did not understand that they were in spiritual warfare against the idolatrous demons of the land. Nor did they realize that their children could be exposed to demonic influence through contact with the inhabitants. They allowed local baby sitters and children of the land to play with their daughter. One of the local boys involved their daughter in "playing doctor." This involved sexual exposure---a factor that demons use. But of course the parents did not understand this. They never spoke to the family about the reality of demons or spiritual warfare. Their daughter became invaded by demons who affected her sexual outlook and behavior. She behaved as a tomboy not properly regarding her femininity. She came to me for counsel, for she knew something was bothering her self-esteem. We tested for demonic influence and found out the story just presented. The Lord led her to confess the childhood sin. Exercising her authority in Christ, she dismissed the wicked spirit affecting her sexuality. The parents would not believe her when she told them of her difficulty and deliverance. Such things, they thought, could not happen to believers. Christians often walk into demonic lands with no idea of how dangerous it is and how they must commit themselves and their children to the Lord for His protection and then be alert to dangers. Several years later I met her as the joyful mother of children.

We would do well to present the unborn to the Lord for His protection even before conception for protection in the womb as well as during birth and after birth. We should ask the Lord to cancel any possible ancestral curses against the children,

In one southern city where I spoke on Satanism to a large group I found out afterward that the head pediatrician at the local hospital was a Satanist who dedicated the newborn babies to his god. In that same city, the high school principal---obviously influential---was also a Satanist. Because there had been suicides and murders in five contiguous counties, Christian business men had invited me and a sheriff's deputy investigating satanic crime to present to those who had been invited to a chicken dinner the real danger and activity of Satanic covens. The deputy presented the evidence. I gave the biblical perspective of Satanism. Even the local press gave this presentation a good evaluation.

Selectivity

Commanders give their soldiers specific assignments for their engagement in the battle.

We have specific commands from the Word of God. We must keep up communications with headquarters.

Check your battle orders found in the Word of God (1 Peter 1:19). Keep up prayer communication with the Lord to keep on track.

For a soldier to follow spurious or non-authentic orders would be disastrous. Refuse any false orders from false teachers or false spirits. They often seem the real thing; but Satan is a counterfeiter, and so are his servants (2 Cor. 11:3, 13--14). There are many hucksters and seemingly good and powerful teachers who would give us good advice. Some deny the operations of Satan and say we have nothing to fear from him. Some regard him as bound in this age and inoperative against God's people. Others would have you rely on special powers to be obtained by following their advice or receiving their treatment. "Do this to get the power of the Holy Spirit," they may say. Beware, because Satan can use the good intentioned but uninstructed as well as the deceivers. Satan's messengers masquerade as angels of light.

Be cautious of false teachers who misuse the Word of God just as did Satan when He tempted Christ (Matt. 4:1--11). The apostle Paul warned against the infiltration of false teachers (1 Tim. 4:1--3). Watch for those who have a "special word from God" in addition to the Bible.

Beware of those who claim special spiritual gifts that make them authorities or give them supernatural insights, or special powers to heal, or unusual powers in prayer. There are many who watch the 700 Club and TV personalities with special powers and are not aware of the dangers of following certain peculiar doctrines or practices. Falling backward after the laying on of hands is not of God. The fruit of the Spirit is self-control.

Beware of going off on your own mission or your own insights without checking with solid biblical advisors. The late gifted Bible teacher, Dr. Harry Ironside, used to say that if he found something he thought to be a new teaching he would wait twenty years before announcing it. During that time he might find out the truth.

These are matters of preparedness---alertness and allegiance. Let me suggest some practical checks we should use in the battle..

Perspectives for the Battle

We need to check on ourselves to make sure we are keeping a good battle plan in our living and praying properly.

Reality Check

We need to ask God to help us see things as they really are to see situations from a proper view.

Regarding Satan's Power

We need to be balanced in our concept of Satan's abilities. He is subject to God and limited; but he has great powers. He is to be respected but not feared.

Don't underestimate his craft and power. Paul commanded the Ephesians to rely upon the Lord's strength and might, because the devil has powerful schemes---well thought out plans of attack (Eph. 6:10). Believers do not always recognize a Satanic set up. He warned the church to forgive the offender who had been disciplined and evidently repented and changed his ways. When he said, "for we are not ignorant of his schemes" (2 Cor. 2:11; purposes, designs) he was not speaking of the Corinthians who were vulnerable. He was speaking of himself and those with him. Paul was warning of Satan's attempt to divide the congregation. To not forgive or retain anger is to give Satan an opportunity (Eph. 4: 26--27).

Satan not only has hidden schemes, but he has a great soldiery. Demons are well experienced and successful accomplices. They are evil, treacherous, and stubbornly tenacious. They have a great track record. And Satan knows how to assign them and use them to prosper his plans. Martin Luther said it: "On earth is not his equal." We are no match for this great evil angel and his hosts.

Don't overestimate his control and power. Satan is a creature. He is God's Satan. God owns him and will limit him as in the case of Job and his affliction. God protected Job and restricted Satan (Job 1:9--12; 2:6). Satan is under God's sovereign control and is no match for Him. We are not dealing with two comparable forces. God will judge Satan at Christ's return and will finally cast him into the eternal Lake of Fire (Matt. 25:41). Satan will get all the punishment that is due him, and the smoke of his torment will rise forever and ever (Rev. 14:9--11; 20:7--10). God guards and protects his own from being engulfed by Satan..

We are to be neither foolish and under-credit Satan and demons, nor are we to be fearful and over- credit them.

Regarding the Saint's Power

We need to have a proper estimate of our human weakness and our divinely delegated authority and power in Christ.

We are not supermen or little god-men. Contrary to the New Age concept, we are not little gods who can control our lives and destiny. We have no strength in ourselves, but our sufficiency is from God (2 Cor. 3:5). "But we have this treasure in earthen vessels, that the surpassing greatness of the power may be of God and not from ourselves" (2 Cor. 4:7). This was Paul's statement in the context of satanic opposition to the gospel.

Our authority is not shared or merged with Christ. He alone has intrinsic, eternal power. We cannot bring Satan and his whole army to their knees. We cannot order him out of this world. We must know the Scriptural picture and God's plan. God has now allowed him to have some freedom to work his schemes. One day the Lord Jesus will cast Satan and his angels into the abyss and from there into the Lake of Fire for his eternal punishment (Rev. 20:1--10).

We do have supernatural, delegated authority. Our authority is granted by the Risen Lord Jesus (Matt. 28:18--20; Eph. 1:19--2:6). He commissioned us and has raised us to a position of authority over all our enemies. We are raised and seated with Christ in the heavenlies far above all authorities of the unseen world. We need not fear them, but face them with the power that Christ supplies. Christ said this authority continues until the end of this age. We do not and can not control all. There will often be opposition and loss (Rev. 2:10; Heb. 11:36--38).

We are to trust and boldly go where Christ sends us (Matt. 10:16--22). In Christ's delegated authority we can handle what we are assigned, and we can gain victory in the battle as God has designed (Rev. 12:11).

Balance Check

Balance in attitude and action are an essential part of the believer's life and warfare.

Recognize the possibility of demonic intervention.

We know that we wrestle not against flesh and blood, but against spiritual forces (Eph. 6:12). These are well organized and well directed demonic powers under Satan. So when in doubt as to whether demonic forces are involved in a particular matter, commit your case to God and pray in this way: "If the enemy has any part in this, Lord, You know. Now we ask You to govern the situation and to let us know what we need to understand. We exercise the authority that You gave us and command demonic forces out of this situation." God understands our lack of knowledge and does not consider our question a lack of faith (James 1:5).

Recognize the possibility of human aspects also.

We suffer physical ailments from natural causes. We suffer mental ailments. Many believers are ill-informed and biased in this area. Mental illnesses may find their root in physical and emotional maladies. Satan is not the cause of all mental illness. However, he may aggravate or fake mental difficulties. But we cannot assign all physical or mental illness to demonic sources.

We suffer human opposition also. The Apostle Paul recognized that (2 Thess. 3:1--2). We need to keep in mind that there may be an overlapping of the physical, the mental, and the demonic. The enemy can affect the body and the mind. We need to have a proper, biblically wholistic approach to our difficulties.

Hope Check

We must put on the helmet of the hope of deliverance in the battle. With God for us, we are on the winning side. To lose sight of that is to drop an essential piece of armor and make ourselves vulnerable to the enemy's attack. We must keep firmly in mind the truth God has set before us.

Remember Christ's Victory.

In His Ministry. Christ overcame the forces of evil in His life. He delivered many who were demon oppressed (Matt. 8:16). This was a proof of His office as Messiah (Matt. 12:28). This is what the apostles preached (Acts 2:22; 10:38). This is what we believe.

By His Commission. Before His ascension He gave authority to His disciples. He gave the Twelve authority over unclean spirits to cast them out (Matt. 10:1). Not only the twelve apostles but also to the seventy messengers returned reporting that demons were subject to them in Christ's name. He reminded them that more important than their authority was their relationship to God. "Nevertheless do not rejoice in this, that the spirits are subject to you, but rejoice that your names are recorded in heaven" (Luke 10:1, 17).

By His Cross. In His death he stripped Satan of his power. The Apostle John writes, "The Son of God appeared for this purpose, that He might destroy the works of the devil" (1 John 3:8). In speaking of His death on the cross, the Lord Jesus declared, "Now judgment is upon this world; now the ruler of this world shall be cast out" (John 12:31-32). Hebrews 2:14-15 reminds us of Christ's becoming genuine man "that through death, He might render powerless him who had the power of death, that is, the devil, and might deliver those who through fear of death were subject to slavery all their lives."

Of Christ, the God-man, Paul states, "When He had disarmed the rulers and authorities, He made a public display of them, having triumphed over them through Him" (Col. 2:15). This is a reference to Christ's death and resurrection which determined the judgment of Satan and the breaking of his power.

By His Coming Again. At the Second Coming Christ will finally dispose of Satan and his hosts. Upon returning Christ will cast Satan into the abyss and shut him in for the 1,000 years of His earthly reign over the earth on David's throne (Rev. 20:1--6). After the 1,000 years are finished, Satan will be let loose to foment a final human and demonic rebellion against the rule of Christ. God sends fire to devour the human rebels and casts "the devil who deceived them . . . into the lake of fire and brimstone where the beast [Antichrist] and the false prophet are also, and they will be tormented day and night forever and ever" (Rev. 20:7--10). There will be no recycling of any evil in the new heavens and the new earth. Death and pain are gone. All that Satan introduced to the human race will be gone forever. Christ will reign in righteousness for eternity (Rev. 21--22)!

Remember the Christian's Victory.

We join Christ in His victory due to our union with Him. But we have responsibilities in the battle. There are things we must do to benefit in our lives now from the Lord's victory.

We must recall key truths. We should review Satan's schemes so that we are no ignorant and caught unaware. We will be encouraged to recall the truth of the Savior's success, His power over Satan during His life on earth, His spoiling Satan by His death on the cross, and His resurrection in power. We can rest in God's love, mercy, and grace, and in His sovereign control of all things.

We must recognize the believer's position in Christ. We have been joined by the baptism of the Holy Spirit to Christ. And in Christ we were legally crucified, raised, and seated with Christ far above all our enemies (Eph. 1:19--2:6). This is our position of victory. Demons do not want us to recognize this, because it means that they must obey us when we exercise our delegated authority

Resist in Christ's authority.

We exercise authority in allegiance to God. We submit to Him and obey His Word. We take on the whole armor of God---the three pieces due to our position and the three pieces supplied in our practice. We follow through with actions of godliness. We trust and obey and live to please God and serve others.

Rely on our Heavenly Father.

Our God is the creator and sustainer of the universe. He is sovereign over all creation, material and spiritual. All creatures are subject to Him and He is in unrivaled control.

We depend on the providence of God. God knows all and cares for all. Not a sparrow falls without Him. All our hairs are numbered. He keeps all stars and planets in their place and sustains them. We can depend on His provision for all we need, for He knows all and intervenes for us. He hears and answers our prayers.

We depend upon the promises of God. His Word forever stands secure. It is settled in heaven and is totally reliable (Ps. 199:89). Those who know the faithfulness of God can say with Joshua that none of His good promises have failed. All have come to pass (Josh. 21:45). All the promises of God in Christ are reliable (2 cor. 1:20). He has promised never ever to leave us and never ever to forsake us (Heb. 13:5). We can rely on our Father to care for us and to back us up in the battle. He is our rock, our fortress, our stronghold, and our deliverer in whom we can take refuge (Ps. 144:1--2).

We depend on the power of God. In all of our life, our struggles, our temptations, and our battles, we can trust in the power of God to sustain us and deliver us. If we know the character and the strength of the God of the Bible---the God of our Lord Jesus Christ---we will be able to trust Him. We need to develop a good concept of God. He is great and good and just and wise. He is faithful and true, loving and kind, full of grace and mercy. He is absolutely sovereign---ruling and overruling. He is the God of the galaxies and the God of genes. He declares, "Behold, I am the LORD, the God of all flesh; is anything to difficult for Me?"(Jer. 32:27). He is a God whom we can trust, a strong tower into whom we may run and be safe (Prov. 18:10). He is also a God who will equip us and enable us for the battle that continues.

Conclusion

We must prepare ourselves for battle with allegiance to the Lord, and alertness to the enemy. We should possess the proper perspective about God's allowing Satan some power and God's delegating believers' authority through their exalted position in Christ. We need biblical balance and positive hope. God has granted us these provisions

If God is for us, who can be against us? We are more than conquerors through Christ!

In view of all we have studied from God's Word about the reality of warfare, the schemes of the enemy, the place of prayer, and the specifics of warfare praying, let us give ourselves to determined prayer to win the well-fought day and bring about the advancement of Christ's cause in our world today to the glory and praise of our Risen Lord Jesus. To Him every knee shall bow, and every tongue shall confess He is Lord of all!

Questions to Ponder

1. Do you think Christians are really alert and ready to act against spiritual evil? How can we become alert?

2. What are some excesses or dangers possible in spiritual warfare praying?

3. Explain the extremes we may find in facing the reality of spiritual warfare?

4. What is the relationship of natural causes and demonic causes of difficulties we may face?

5. What positive concepts and promises must we remember when facing the enemy in prayer?

PART II
Pattern Warfare Prayers

CHAPTER 6

Psalms for Warfare

Let me suggest several types of prayers that can serve as patterns for your personal warfare praying. The exact words are not required. The principles are important. You can make these your own prayers or create similar ones. The imprecatory prayers in which the psalmist asks God regarding his enemies are patterns for us.

The psalmists often pray against their enemies often considering their enemies to be God's enemies. Listen to the bold language that King David used:

> O that Thou wouldst slay the wicked, O God;
> Depart from me, therefore, men of bloodshed.
> For they speak against Thee wickedly,
> And Thine enemies take *Thy name* in vain.
> Do not I hate those who hate Thee, O LORD?
> And do I not loathe those who rise up against Thee?
> I hate them with the utmost hatred;
> They have become my enemies. (Ps. 139:19--22)

We can take such psalms as inspired patterns for our warfare praying. David knew that spiritual forces were behind his human enemies just as we have been informed (Dan. 10:13, 20; Eph. 6:10--12). We can read what are called "imprecatory psalms" as specific prayers against our spiritual enemies. Let me suggest several other such prayers in the book of Psalms.

> Depart from me, all you who do iniquity, for the LORD has heard the voice of my weeping. The LORD has heard my supplication, the LORD receives my prayer. All my enemies shall be ashamed and greatly dismayed; they shall turn back, they shall suddenly be ashamed (Ps. 6:8--10).

> Arise, O LORD, in thine anger; lift up Thyself against the rage of my adversaries. And arouse Thyself for me; Thou hast appointed judgment . . . Vindicate me, O LORD, according to my righteousness and my integrity that is in me. O let the evil of the wicked come to an end, but establish the righteous . . . My shield is with God, who saves the upright in heart (Ps. 7:6--10).

> Arise, O LORD, confront him, bring him low; deliver my soul from the wicked with Thy sword. (Ps. 17:13).

> But as for me, I trust in Thee, O LORD. I say, "Thou art my God." My times are in Thy hand; deliver me from the hand of my enemies, and from those who persecute me . . . Let me not be put to shame, O LORD, for I call upon Thee; let the wicked be put to shame, let them be silent in Sheol (Ps. 31:14--17).

> Thou art my King, O God; command victories for Jacob. Though Thee we will push back our

adversaries; through Thy name we will trample down those who rise up against us (Ps. 44:4--5).

Deliver me from my enemies, O my God; set me *securely* on high, away from these who rise up against me. Deliver me from those who do iniquity, and save me from men of bloodshed. . . . Awake to punish all the nations; do not be gracious to any who *are* treacherous in iniquity
(Ps.59:5).

O give us help against the adversary, for deliverance by man is in vain. Through God we shall do valiantly, and it is He who will tread down our adversaries (Ps. 60:11).

O God, do not be far from me; O my God, hasten to my help! Let those who are adversaries of my soul be ashamed consumed; let them be covered with reproach and dishonor who seek to injure me. But as for me, I will hope continually, and will praise Thee yet more and more (Ps. 71:12--14).

These are but a few of the psalms that give us patterns of warfare praying that we do well to follow. I suggest that you read through the book of Psalms and count the number of psalms that involve prayer against enemies. I think you will be surprised at the percentage of the 150 psalms that specifically pray in this fashion.

Some might wonder how this aligns with the Lord Jesus' telling us that we should pray for our enemies and those who despitefully use us. I suggest that the Lord was speaking about our personal human enemies whom we were to treat respectfully and seek their good and not condemning them. But the imprecatory psalms pray against fixed and determined enemies of God. Since demons will not and cannot repent nor change their ways, demonic forces certainly are not to be forgiven. God will judge them. Though the psalmist is often praying against human enemies, the principles apply to spiritual warfare against Satan and demons. The writers knew of the opposition from the spirit world. It was all around them. Idolatrous worship involved the worship of demons whom their enemies revered and on whom they relied (Ps.106:35--38). We can certainly pray against evil spiritual forces knowing that Christ is backing us with His authority.

Questions to Ponder

1. Explain some of the features of the imprecatory psalms---the psalms that pray against enemies. How could you use any of these psalms as you pray?

2. How do your reconcile praying against enemies with Christ's urging us to pray for our enemies?

3. Why would God have us pray against fixed and determined enemies?

4. Why do you think God never commands us to pray for fallen angels?

CHAPTER 7

Prayers for Personal Freedom

The following are scripturally based pattern prayers. They have no power in themselves. The exact wording is not all that important though the words are carefully chosen. They carry no magical formulae that guarantee success. They express complete dependence on the true and living God to hear and to answer according to His wise and gracious will. Many have found great relief in adopting these prayers as their very own and praying them sincerely to the Father in Jesus' authority. May they be of great help to you, your family, and your friends.

I would suggest that as you pray these prayers you mark in the margin the points at which you find pointed meaning in your life. Mark also those points where you find distraction or opposition for clues as to what specific things you might be battling.

Recognizing the Reality of Spiritual Warfare

Heavenly Father, the Father of our Lord Jesus Christ, our Savior who died for our sins and whom you raised from the dead, I come to You in His name. I recognize the reality of spiritual warfare and my involvement in the battle with Satan and his demons. I ask You to strengthen me with your great power that I may be able to stand against the schemes of the enemy, for I recognize that we do not battle merely with humans but with spiritual beings with power beyond my ability to withstand.

In your pattern prayer, Lord Jesus, You told us to pray that we not be led into temptation where the Evil One would be able to overcome us. Now that I have a better understanding of the battle in which I'm engaged and of the dangers involved I recognize my responsibility and cast myself upon You to make me vigilant and to enable me to stand in the resources You have provided.

Therefore I take the full armor that You have supplied. Thank You for the protection provided by depending upon the truth centered in You, Lord. Thank You for the righteousness you have granted me through faith in your great sacrifice on my behalf. Thank You also for the peace that is mine through the gospel even in the midst of battle. I now take up that solid shield of confidence in You and in your Word. I put on the helmet of the certainty of deliverance in the battle, for in You I am on the winning side. I also take with me the sharp sword of the sayings of the Word of God that are appropriate to my need and my opposition. I will pray depending on the Holy Spirit against the forces of evil and for the victory of righteousness.

I choose to submit to God and resist the devil that he would be defeated in my life and the life of my family. Teach me to pray as I should in total dependence on You. Amen.

Protection from the Forces of Evil

I ask You, Lord God, to protect me, my family, and my church against the assaults of the devil and his demons. I am confident that You are for me and no one can be successful against me as I walk in dependence and obedience. Let me to stand firm in the truth in Christ and to follow your leading in my life. I renounce all self-sufficiency and pride and humbly depend upon You. Teach me what I need to know about the Christian life in the Spirit and about the reality of spiritual warfare. Make me aware of the first approach of the enemy and enable me to resist him in the faith. Help me to confess my sins and my weakness and to command him to back down and go where the risen Lord Jesus sends him.

I go confidently forward with You, Lord Jesus; for You are my strength, my fortress, and the Victor over sin, the world, and Satan. I take my position as victor in the Victorious Lord, and I will trust and obey. I pray in the powerful name of the risen and living Savior. Amen.

Freedom from Demonic and Occult Bondage

The following prayers are suggested patterns for specific and effective warfare praying for freedom from occult and demonic bondage. There is no power in the exact words. We are children and soldiers petitioning our wise, gracious, and powerful Heavenly Father for what He would think best for us. We also recognize the reality of spiritual warfare and ask the Lord to act in our behalf as we take our stand for His righteousness and against all forms of evil in our lives and around us.

Affirming Position in Christ

My great and gracious Heavenly Father, I worship You and praise You for who You are. You are the creator, sustainer, providential controller of the universe and of my life. You sent your Son, the Lord Jesus, to take away our sins. I believe that He is fully God and fully man without sin, that He is the only mediator between God and men, that He lived a sinless life and taught us your truth, that He died in my place to give to You a complete satisfaction for my sins, and that You enabled me to come to Him in faith for the full forgiveness of my sins.

I take my stand in Christ. I believe that the Holy Spirit baptized me into Christ that very moment I first trusted Christ as my Savior. I now stand complete in Christ. By your strong, saving grace, I now have perfect acceptance in the righteousness of Christ. I have perfect access to your throne of grace in any time of need. I have provided authority to carry on the work You have assigned to me---even to face Satan and his demons and to pray and work against them. Amen.

Pledge of Allegiance

On the basis of my position in Christ and realizing that all that I am and have is a grace gift from Your hand, I yield my whole being---spirit and body---to You as a reasonable and loving response. I choose to submit to Your will and way in my life. I stand against the sinful capacity that resides within me and count myself truly dead to sin and genuinely alive to God through my union with Christ. I also count myself as crucified to the world and its lusts and count the world as crucified to me. I believe that Christ died, rose, and was exalted at the right hand of God the Father far above all angelic beings good and evil. I count myself as raised and seated with Him in the heavenly places far above my spiritual enemies. I stand against these demonic enemies in the righteousness and authority of the risen and exalted Savior.

I declare my position of victory over these enemies just as Christ stands over them. I choose this day whom I shall serve. I will serve the Lord Jesus Christ and the Triune God. You and You alone, O Triune God, are worthy of worship and praise. You and You alone are worthy of cultivating my life. I commit my entire mind, my emotions, my will, my needs, my hopes, my relationships, and my works to you. Work in my life by the Holy Spirit to will and accomplish all your good pleasure. Give me a heart to follow You completely. Keep me in the way of righteous for your name's sake, and enable me to stand for You and serve You all of my life. I pray this in the name of the Son of God. Amen.

Standing against Ancestral Influences

Realizing that the Second Commandment promises to the generational line the blessings of obedient ancestors and the curses of idolatrous and disobedient ancestors I ask You, Lord Jesus, to break and cancel all the curses and evil effects of the sins of my ancestors. Free me and my family from demonic influences that accompany idolatry and controlling sins.

I may not know what evil or sinful matters my ancestors practiced; but if any of them were involved in any form of idolatry, false religion, witchcraft, Satanism, illicit or immoral behaviors that have affected me or my family, I confess those things are evil and ask You to forgive and cancel their effects upon us. If there were ceremonies, sacrifices, or dedications of children made by any one inside or outside against the family, membership in secret societies---such as Masons---I stand against these and ask You to free me and my family from these influences.

I thank You that You hear and answer me in this matter and will free me from the power and bondages ancestral sins may have brought into my life. You, Lord Jesus, came to set the prisoners free and to heal the brokenhearted. Amen.

Renouncing Personal Occult Practices

Holy Father, whatever involvement I have had in the occult I totally and specifically renounce as opposed to your person and your commands. I confess that I have by such sought hidden knowledge and secret power. By so much I judged that You, your truth, and your provision were not sufficient for me. I recognize this as rebellion and idolatry, and I choose against it.

Any form of divination in which I dabbled I confess and stand against. I reject involvement with any of the following: *ouija* board, tarot (predictive) cards, palm reading, tea leaf reading, astrology, ESP, predictive dreams, repeated *deja vu* experiences, visiting psychics or fortune tellers.

If I have practiced magic or sought to control persons or things through "mind control," I confess this and stand against it as sin. Any love or hate magic, any binding or loosing, any hurt or healing ceremonies, any attempts to move objects or control circumstances---all these I reject as contrary to trusting in the true and living God. I confess and renounce fantasy games (as D&D). Whatever contact I may have sought with spirits---either the human dead or with guiding spirits---I confess and renounce this as trafficking with demons and contrary to the commands of God. Any advantage I may have gained through such, I renounce and forsake. If I have listened to mediums or channelers, I reject this practice as rebellion against God, the Creator. If I have gained any advantage through such, I refuse to use it or continue in it.

Whatever involvement I have had with witchcraft or Satanism I confess as wretched sin. I renounce any sacrifice, any dedication, any ceremonies linking me to the gods that such people serve. I ask You, True and Living God, to cleanse and free me from such connections and control. I declare myself free from these.

Thank You, my Heavenly Father, that You are sufficient for me and that You care for me. I cast all my cares upon You and trust You for all my needs. I admit that I do not have the wisdom or the power to stand on my own. Instead of seeking to overcome my limitations by resorting to sinful practices, I will turn to You with all my weaknesses for all my needs. I will trust You and You alone. Thank you for forgiveness and for removing this ground from the enemy. Amen.

Renouncing Improper Treatment Received

Loving and gracious Father, if I have been treated suspiciously or improperly by anyone who may have had occult or demonic powers, I ask You to free me from any evil influence in my life that may have resulted.

I confess and renounce the following: having been hypnotized, being been magically healed, allowing my mind to be read, having my astrology chart cast, having my eyes read (iridology) or having hands laid on me to receive a special gift---tongues, prophecy, discernment, power. I was wrong to have allowed these things.

If I allowed any improper sexual touch or sexual union outside of marriage, I confess that as a violating of your laws, holy Father, and a violation of the sanctity of my body which You have bought for your holy purposes.

If I have allowed someone to lead me through vows or dedications as in secret societies, I renounce those vows and ask You to free me from any resulting bondage.

I thank you that You are the designer of life and the provider of all that I need. Forgive me for these matters confessed. I take my stand against the enemy who would take advantage of me through such sins. I trust You to remove the enemy's ground and declare it to be gone. Amen.

Renouncing Improper Attitudes

I thank You, my wise and gracious Father, that You created me in your image so that I am a person who can have fellowship with You---to think, feel, and choose with You. Forgive me for thinking improperly of myself or of others also made in your image. This has interfered with personal growth and interpersonal relationships. I confess that poor self-esteem that says I am a "nobody" that should be ignored and rejected. I reject an unhealthy view of my mind or my body that would lead me to mistreat myself or hate myself. In doing so I hate someone that You love and have bought at the awful price of Your Son's death. You don't make junk, and You don't buy junk. I accept myself---my person, my mind, my sexuality, my body with all its features--- because You have wonderfully designed and fashioned me just as I am apart from the damage I may have inflicted. I thank you for the way You have made me in every detail.

Forgive me for thinking unfittingly of my person or my body. I reject any thoughts of suicide and any ideas of mistreating myself. If I have allowed depression and self-pity to rule my mind, I confess and reject this as sin. I recognize there may be reasons for depression that I cannot control. For these I ask proper help and counsel. But for that which I can control I give myself to You for strength and healing.

Thank You, Holy Father, for graciously giving me freedom from these improper and degrading thoughts. I trust You to change my attitudes. You are able. Amen.

Renouncing Improper Personal Actions

Holy Father, I recognize your claims upon my mind and body. Therefore I confess and renounce any personal practice that was deviation from or transgression of the will of God. I reject any involvement with drugs, alcohol, illicit sex, mind-control techniques, TM, martial arts, psychic healing, new age practices, false religions, cults, or sects. I confess any attempts to mistreat myself or any misuse of my body in improper display. I confess and renounce any use of masturbation, and I reject the fantasy that this involves. I confess any mistreatment of other persons.

I stand against Satan and his demons that would seek to use these practices as inroads, and I claim my freedom in Christ from any control and bondage that might have resulted. Thank You, Lord Jesus, for coming to destroy the works of the devil and his hosts. Amen.

Renouncing Doubt and Fear

Since You are thoroughly and forever trustworthy, O Living God, I renounce doubt and fear as incompatible with our relationship established by You upon my faith in the crucified, risen, and exalted Lord Jesus the Messiah. You have told us not to be anxious, for You care for us intimately and constantly. I would continually cast all my concerns upon You, for You always are concerned about me. Forgive me for fear and anxiety, and teach your weak and failing child to trust in You always.

Forgive me for doubting your love, your care, and your Word in the Scriptures. You have given us all that we need for life and godliness in this present world. Doubt has led me astray to seek other than your best for my life---in jobs, relationships, achievements and pleasures. I reject trusting in myself, my resources, my plans, my friends instead of trusting in my all-powerful Father. Nothing can separate me from your love---neither death nor life, Satan nor demons, things present nor future, height nor depth, time nor space, nor any created thing. I am yours forever, and You are mine.

Whatever ground I may have given to the enemy in these things I claim back in the powerful name of the Risen God-man. Help me to reject instantly any attempt by the enemy to introduce doubt or fear to my mind. Amen.

Renouncing Rebellion

Good and gracious Father, I recognize that rebellion against You originally came from Satan. I also realize that I tend to rebel against You through my own sinful capacities. I confess and renounce all attitudes and practices of rebellion in my life. I will not allow this satanic practice and influence to continue in my life. You alone are worthy of praise and trust and obedience. I give myself to You this day and every day for all You have for me---the good, pleasing, and perfect will of God. Work in me to trust and obey.

Forgive me for rebellion against all rightly constituted human authority in home, school, church, and government. Teach me and help me to submit properly to God-established authorities.

Where I have submitted to improperly constituted authorities, siding with them, participating with them, fearing them, forgive me. I reject submission to false teachers, false religious leaders, and false doctrine. I claim the forgiveness and cleansing that You promised on the basis of the blood of Christ. Amen.

Renouncing Pride and Self-Promotion

Lord Jesus, I thank You that You did not retain all the glory and privileges that were rightfully yours in heaven but that You became a genuine human and humble servant to do the will of Your Father God. For this God highly honored You and gave You the name above every name in heaven and earth. You deserve honor and glory from all whom You have redeemed. You have redeemed me by your precious blood. Therefore I humble myself before You that You may gain honor and glory from my life.

I renounce all pride and self-promotion as unfitting to our relationship. I realize that Satan fell through selfish ambition and pride. I don't want to side with the enemy. I humbly acknowledge that I have no good thing in my human resources and that I am unable to do any good apart from your enabling grace. Apart from your saving grace, I deserve the fire of hell. Even now that I am through faith in Christ in Your grace I am an unprofitable servant at my best. But what I am designed to be, I will be by the grace of God. Take my life and make it a trophy of your love and grace. Help me to be your servant and the servant of Christ to others whom You love. I abhor pride and choose humility. I will walk in dedication and determination to honor Christ and serve others. In Jesus' name I pray. Amen.

Renouncing All Bitterness and Grudges

Holy and gracious Father, I realize that your Word tells us to put away all anger, bitterness, and evil speaking and that we are to forgive grievances we may have against others just as You have forgiven us in Christ. I recognize that I may not have totally forgiven those who have offended me. I may still retain some bitterness in my heart against them whether family, friends, or opponents. Sometimes I might want to retaliate against them, but I choose to follow your command. They may not apologize, but I do forgive any who I think have wronged me by turning my case over to You. I will not retain my anger or thoughts of revenge but allow You to deal with them properly. I am not qualified. You are the Judge.

If I am able and it is appropriate, I will seek reconciliation. I realize that may not always be possible or proper, but I seek your direction and enablement. I will not seek to exercise my power by retaining my anger, and I refuse to let bitterness continue. You have warned that if such anger continues, we give opportunity to the devil. I take my stand against the sin of lack of forgiveness. I also take my stand against Satan and ask You to free me from his power exercised because of my sin in this area. If anger seeks to return, I will remind myself before You that I have turned the matter over to You for your adjudication. I realize that long standing hurts don't disappear overnight. Protect me from the enemy's tactics that would continue to remind me and to condemn me. I trust You to handle my mind and my emotions in these matters. Give me a patient, loving, gracious spirit in my attitudes and dealings with others. Amen.

Standing in the Power and Armor of God---A Summary Prayer

Father God, You have warned us that we do not wrestle against humans but against forces under Satan. I would come to You for your power and strength in the battle. Enable me to stand in the power that You supply in Christ. I will not trust in my power not even in my prayers. My strength is from You, Lord. My hope is in You, Lord. See me through to victory.

I would as You have commanded put on the full armor that You supply. These pieces I would put on in full confidence that they are sufficient for the battle. I know that even if there are difficult times, stresses, set-backs, and even some defeats, You are the Victor, Lord Jesus; and I am victor by virtue of my union with You. You will enable me to gain the victory in practical ways in the fray. I will stand clothed with the armor You supply for the heat of the battle.

Therefore, setting aside all sin, pride, self-sufficiency, and error, I would put on the whole armor of God. I recognize that through my position in the grace of Christ I already have on the first three pieces of armor. I thank You for the belt of truth---that I stand in the truth system that centers in the person and work of Christ. I thank You that I have the breastplate of righteousness---that I stand in the righteousness of Christ which has been placed on my account through justification by faith. I thank You that I have the sandals of peace---that I stand in peace with God through faith in Christ. Even in the midst of the battle I know God is for me and will help me because of my eternal relationship to Him through the blood of Christ.

I now take up the other three pieces of armor You have provided for my action. I raise the shield of faith---that great defense of confidence in your person and Word. With it I will ward off all the doubts and threats that the enemy would fire at me. I put on the helmet of salvation---that protection of hope of deliverance in the battle. I am on the winning side. God will triumph. Satan will be defeated. I can trust the living Lord in all my circumstances. I now pick up the sword of the Spirit---the sayings of the Word of God that are appropriate to my need in the battle. Your Word is true and I depend on it. I will hide it in my heart and use it boldly against all error to cut through all falsehood and opposition.

With the power of Christ and the armor of God I stand complete. I determine by your power and grace to stand firm in all areas and events of life. I will trust You and You alone to care for my well-being, safety, freedom, and development.

Again I affirm my trust in the Lord Jesus as the Risen Savior Lord and Victor over all evil. I confess and renounce all that dishonors Christ and hinders my relationship to You and my service for You. I submit to you. I resist the devil. I trust You to make Him flee from me. Grant me deliverance from any influences and any control that Satan and his demons might seek to exercise over me. My mind, my emotions, my will, my body---my whole being---is yours, Lord Jesus. Break the bondage of sin and evil and set me free to live for your honor and glory. I praise You for your goodness, grace, love, and power and believe that You will continue to deliver me and cultivate my life in your good and sovereign plan. Amen.

Prayer for Freedom from Oppression

I confess and renounce any ancestral sins affecting me. I cancel the ground they have been using, and command them to depart to face the Lord Jesus.

I confess and renounce all personal sins that have given the enemy ground (moral occasion). I cancel that ground and command all associated spirits to depart to where the true Lord Jesus sends them.

I confess and cancel any ground given by transfer of wicked spirits to me by any control over my mind or body. I confess and renounce any way that I may have allowed that. I reject any control that was forced upon me and declare myself free from that influence. I also break any evil soul ties---emotional bondages---to those who violated my privacy and dignity. I command any wicked spirits that transferred to me to depart to face the Lord Jesus

On the basis of my union with Christ and assuming my authority granted to me in the risen Savior, I command in Jesus' name all wicked spirits within or around me to depart and to go where the true Lord Jesus sends them. I give You thanks and praise, Lord Jesus, Son of God, for your grace, love, and power. Accomplish all your will in my life. Set me free from bondage and heal me of all that the enemy and his agents have brought upon me. Amen.

Questions to Ponder

1. How does your position in Christ relate to your warfare praying?

2. Why do we first need to pray for our own freedom before praying for others?

3. Why should we pray against ancestral bondage and influences?

4. Did you notice any hesitancy or confusion in praying any of these prayers?

5. Why do you suppose there might have been some opposition? How will you handle this?

CHAPTER 8

Prayer for Personal Needs

Besides the following prayers there are suggested prayers in the previous section that deal with personal needs as well. We start with prayer for ourselves so that we might ready to pray for others.

Prayer for the Filling of the Holy Spirit

Father God, the Father of our Lord Jesus Christ, I come to You in Jesus' name that I might be filled with the true Holy Spirit. I ask You to rule out every influence of demonic forces and to enable me to pray with clarity of mind and uninterrupted understanding. I confess that I have sought my own way and attempted to acquire acceptance, power, and control. I have quenched and grieved the Spirit and walked in the flesh.

I now count myself legally dead to sin, separated from the domination of the sin nature. I count myself joined to Christ in His death, resurrection, and ascension and am seated legally with Him in the heavenlies. I now yield my whole being, my mind and members of my body to You, my Heavenly Father, and ask you to fill me and cultivate me by the Holy Spirit. Enable me to live to please You in every aspect of my life and to exhibit the fruit of the Spirit to honor and glorify You. I ask the Holy Spirit to teach me the Word of God, to make the Lord Jesus real to me, and to help me live a life free from legalism and license and full of love.

I humbly submit this request to You with thanks for your answer in the name of your Son. Amen.

Prayer for the Salvation of Others

Father, I recognize that there are barriers that hinder the unsaved from trusting Christ. I recognize that Satan blinds their minds and that natural blindness also keeps them from understanding and receiving the gospel. I know that You are gracious and sovereign and that You turn unbelievers to the Savior. So I pray for enlightenment so that the person for whom I am concerned might come to hear the gospel through an effective contact---a person to share or some accurate media message. I also pray also that the Lord of the Harvest would send messengers at an appropriate time (Rom. 10:13--17). I pray for the removal of satanic blinding and demonic deception. I pray also for conviction by the Holy Spirit. I ask specifically for the clarification of sin, righteousness, and judgment, and the necessity of trusting in Christ (John 16:7--11). I ask that the Spirit would convince the unbeliever that the gospel is true and applies to him/her and that he/she is responsible to trust the Savior. I pray for God the Father to draw that person to come to Christ; for Jesus said, "No one can come to Me, unless the Father who sent Me draw him" (John 6:44). Amen

We can not guarantee the salvation of anyone by these prayers, but we can trust our gracious and righteous God to do his will. Many will respond as we pray in this biblical fashion. God is sovereign and gracious, merciful, and kind. We ought at all times to pray and not to lose heart" (Luke 18:1).

Prayer for Physical Healing

Recognizing that we are in spiritual warfare, I pray for relief from physical maladies. Thank You for the privilege of praying in the authority that the Lord Jesus gives those joined to Him. Heavenly Father, ruler of all, I commit my physical, emotional, and spiritual welfare to You for your healing and protection. Please intervene specifically on my behalf to break the power of this ailment I am battling. If it is natural, I trust You to personally and directly touch me with the healing I need. If the enemy is taking advantage of this to further the disease or to torture me with the disease, I ask You to break his power and activity along this line and in any way he would seek to oppose my healing. If he had any part in originating this disease, I ask You to judge him directly and severely and to undo any damage he has accomplished. I confess any fear that keeps me from trusting You. I come against discouragement, depression, and despair in the name of the risen Savior; and I ask You to encourage my heart and mind. I cancel whatever ground the enemy thinks he has, and I command him in the authority of Christ to leave me and to go where Jesus sends him.

If there is any part of me (DID) hurting and confused because of trauma experienced, I ask You, Heavenly Father, to comfort and heal that part or those parts and to invite them to come to You for your healing. Break any curse or program designed to ruin me, to disable me, or to harm me in any way and to set your protective guard about me to keep from further damage or affliction. I am your child, and You are my God; and I am trusting You to answer me and to show yourself powerful and sufficient for my needs and that of my family. I trust You to answer this prayer in the way that is pleasing to You. Whatever You have planned for me, give me grace to trust You. I pray in the name of the risen Jesus and for the glory of His name. Amen.

Prayer for Marriages and Families

Father God, You established marriage and blessed it right from the beginning. You are concerned about the inroads Satan has made into marriage and family relationships. He injected his lies into the first marriage and has sought to disrupt and ruin marriage ever since then. I pray that your design for marriage may reign in the Church and in society. You have revealed in your Word that You hate adultery and homosexuality while loving the persons involved. I ask that Satan's perversion may be hindered and many trapped in such relationships would be delivered. May those who teach and preach be bold to share God's truth and minister in love to those in sexual sins. Remove Satan's blinding from the minds of those involved and lead them away from any perversion into God's good and gracious life. May the courts of the land judge according to your truth. Protect us from litigation for our speaking against homosexuality. Only You can bring this about, and I pray that You will. Help us to make our home a haven of love and security and enable us to rear our children in godly fashion. I ask in Jesus' name. Amen.

For Marriages in Trouble

Loving and gracious Father, You have wonderfully designed us male and female. Evolution could not have begun to accomplish what You have created. I pray for my marriage that seems to have hit a rocky road. There are misunderstandings and hard feelings. Forgive me for my shortcomings and overstepping in our relationship. If in any way I have been unfaithful, in mind or body, forgive me. Help me to forgive my spouse and my spouse to forgive me. Help me to love as I ought. In the name of Jesus I cancel the ground I have given to Satan. I command him to leave to where Jesus sends him and his host. I want the relationships that would please You. I can't bring this about, but I ask the Holy Spirit to enable me to speak and relate as I should. I submit our spiritual and physical relationship to You that we might enjoy your blessing. I pray that You would meet the needs of my spouse. I pray that each one of us would recognize your good and gracious will for our marriage and that my dear one would and recognize and trust my love. Help us both to be faithful and true. I pray in the name of our Savior. Amen.

For Troubled or Rebellious Children

I know that Satan and his demons hate my children. I know that You love them and would have them enjoy godly relationships to You and to their parents. Destroy the work of the enemies in direct and in social pressures put upon them. You have given children as gifts to be reared in the nurture and admonition of the Lord so that they may take their place as mature persons contributing to the Church and society. Give wisdom and strength for accomplishing your best in this. For those who are troubled or rebellious we ask us to give us love and firmness to respect, encourage, affirm, warn, and restrain as needed. Bring them back to submission to You and to us in godly fashion. I ask You to break all ancestral evil influences against them. I pray for the destruction of evil societal and peer pressures acting against them. Please lead our children to honor You and to walk in your ways, listening to good advice, and avoiding pitfalls and controlling sins. I commit them to You for your best in their lives. Help me and my spouse to be what we should be to them. In the name of the Lord Jesus I pray. Amen.

For Problems with Addictions

Father God, You who watch over to provide, protect, and guide your children, I pray against the enemy's work in promoting addictions of any sort in my life and in members of my family.

You have told us that we should not become slaves to any habit or practice. We belong to You and our bodies are the temple of the Triune God. We are not to defile or subject our bodies to any power. So I confess and renounce any involvement in alcohol or drugs that have controlled my mind and body. I resist in your power any avarice and the desire for illicit sexual satisfaction or possessions to give me improper pleasure. I take back the moral ground I have given to the devil, resist him, and tell him and his demons to depart to where the Lord Jesus sends them. I commit my heart and mind to Christ and ask Him to relieve me of any addiction that keeps me from enjoying a growing personal relationship to You. Release me (or family members) from Satan's power and allow me to live in the freedom for which Christ bought me. I seek satisfaction and peace only in the Lord Jesus. I pray in the authority of the risen Savior. Amen.

Prayer against Sexual Perversions

Wise and sovereign Lord God, You have created us in your image---persons who can fellowship and think, feel, and choose with You. You made us male and female. Help us to appreciate your marvelous design in sexuality---the complexities of which we cannot totally understand. You also designed marriage as the proper expression of the mating aspect of sexuality. You command us to limit that expression to legitimate marriage of one man and one woman together for a lifetime. I read that when the human race turned from the worship of the true God to idols that sexual perversion was one of the results. I renounce the concepts that I was born homosexual or that I am the opposite sex trapped within my body. I thank You that You planned for me just as I am but want me free from perversion and sin. Help me to live free as the sexual being that You created me to be. I claim my legitimate sexuality and freedom in Christ. If I have practiced any deviation in premarital or extramarital sin with male, female, or any animal, I confess that and renounce it as heinous and claim your forgiveness and cleansing. I commit myself to You, the living God. I ask You to deliver me from such perversions by the authority of crucified and risen Savior. I command all spirits promoting perverted sex to leave me and to go where the Lord Jesus sends them. Amen.

Prayer against Pornography

A recent Christian poll found that both men and woman are definitely drawn to pornography---a five billion dollar per year (at least) industry. The figures show than 56 % of women twenty-five and under seek out porn, and 27% of young adults twenty-five to thirty years first viewed porn before puberty. In our present society porn is considered morally neutral. More than 50 % of senior pastors and youth pastors find that their own battle with pornography has affected their spiritual life and ministry. We need to pray against this plague. In my forty-six years of counseling those having demonic oppression, I have found that demons are involved with such attraction and slavery. Jesus warned against the fornication involved in lust and mental images. Such thoughts are always involved with pornography. I suggest the following type prayer against such involvement.

I thank you, our Creator and Redeemer, that You designed sexuality and its expression as a good and holy creation. You designed intimate sexual relationships to find proper expression within God-designed marriage. You judge sexual violation severely. You hate the perversions found in false religions. I pray for marriages in my acquaintance and those in the church that they may be found in the way of righteousness. I pray against the human and demonic forces involved in pornography and for deliverance and freedom through the name of the Lord Jesus. I pray for those I know who are involved with pornography that they might recognize this improper and perverted concept and control by the enemy. If I am having difficulty along this line, I confess my sin, cancel the moral occasion I have given to Satan, and command him and his demons to leave to the place where Jesus sends them. Help me to take a firm stand against this violation or your good design, against this devaluation of honorable sexual powers, and against interference with good marital relationships. I pray this in Jesus' powerful and holy name. Amen.

Prayer against Self-Stimulation

Many---even some Christian counselors---see nothing wrong with masturbation. In reality it is a perversion of our God-given sexual powers. It almost always involves sexual imagery that is sinful. The Lord Jesus said that if a person lusts after another, that person has committed fornication in the heart. How can masturbation then be a God-given form of relief? In my years of counseling, I have found that demons take advantage of this perversion and drive people to bondage to the habit. It also fosters guilt and shame. Those who do not recognize the reality and scope of spiritual warfare will dismiss this reality. I suggest this prayer.

Holy God and Father, you know what is good and the best for us. You gave us the gift of sex. Help me to recognize the sin and degradation involved in masturbation. It may make me feel good for a short while, but I often end up ashamed and feeling guilty. I confess my sin and helplessness. I ask you to free me from this bondage. I cancel the ground I gave to Satan and command his demons to leave and go where Jesus sends them. Help me to take a firm stand against this scheme of the enemy who would drag me into degradation and shame. I want to live for You and commit all my mind and body to You in Jesus' powerful name. Amen.

C. Fred Dickason, Th. D.

Prayer for the Workplace

Lord Jesus Christ, Great Son of God in whom I trust for my salvation and eternal life, I thank You for your love and sovereign grace in my life in my salvation and at this present time. I trust You for your concerned intervention in the affairs of my life. I trust You for my well being, my relationships, my family, my responsibilities, and my daily needs.

I thank You for the work You have given me to do and for the employment I have. Help me to contribute to the prospering of those for whom I work. Help me to do all that I do as unto You, for You are my Lord and Master who is in charge of my life and my labor. May I continue to work at this place for the benefit of my employers, for my fellow employees, and for my financial benefit as long as it pleases You. I trust You for the course of my life and labor, for I am your child through Jesus Christ.

Great Shepherd of the sheep, watch over me in this workplace that I may be a testimony to You and your truth and grace. Let my attitude be that of serving You in all I do. I am concerned about certain evidences and manifestations of evil in this place, and so I bring this request to You. May the forces of evil be routed and their purposes brought to ruin. Destroy the works of the devil in this place. Do not allow the continuation of misuse of authority, lines of communication, and the misuse of funds. Bring conviction by the Holy Spirit to those not in line with your will. Bring to the minds of those in final authority any improper behavior so that correction may take place. Defeat the schemes of Satan and demons and protect your people that work here. Let your angels attend and protect me and my testimony in this place. Give me grace, patience, and determination to serve You while I wait for your intervention. Empower me to be a witness to the grace of God and the gospel of the Lord Jesus Christ. I would appreciate your acting quickly to alleviate the difficulties that are present here.

I submit my requests to You in the authority that You have given me as joined to the crucified, risen, and exalted victorious Savior. I thank You for hearing me and answering me according to your wise, gracious, and sovereign will. Amen.

Prayer Regarding the Possible Gift of Tongues

No matter what your view is on the appropriateness of the "gift of tongues" for today, the yielded believer should be open to praying this prayer in trusting the exalted and gift-granting Lord to reveal the truth. One thing that we have found is helpful is this type of prayer which is in line with what the Holy Spirit said in 1 John 4:1--3.

Lord Jesus, true Son of God, I ask You regarding my experience with tongues, prophecy, or special insight. If it was not of You---and You obviously know the answer---I ask that You would remove this influence from me and allow me to see your truth in the matter. I trust You in this, for you have completely accepted me in Christ apart from any of my works or gifts. I depend upon your Word for the assurance of my salvation and my development in grace. And if this tongue or prophecy or insight is a deception from demonic forces, I reject them and command them to leave me and to go where Jesus sends them. I pray in the name of the risen Christ. Amen.

Prayer against Passivity

Believers will often confess their sin, and some will cancel the ground given to the devil in their sin; but few will actually command the enemy to leave to where Jesus sends them. There may be several reasons for this omission. They may be unaware of their position and authority provided by Christ. They may afraid to exercise that authority, because it seems strange or foolish. They may be afraid to speak directly to demons fearing the demons' power instead of trusting the victorious Lord. Or they might be afraid of retaliation not realizing the Lord will protect them. Fear is the devil's big tool. We could pray in this fashion:

Sovereign Lord Jesus, I confess my fear and the passivity it instills. I cancel the ground given to the enemy through this and command him to cease his activity against me. I commit my life and well being to You, the risen and conquering Son of God. I assume the provided authority granted to me by my union with You to gain the freedom that You bought for me in your death, resurrection, and exaltation. Help me to face courageously life's demands and to assume boldly and humbly my personal responsibilities. Amen.

Prayer against House Haunting

Often people report strange noises, ghost-like appearances, hearing invisible footsteps, moving of objects, or eerie feelings in certain parts of the house. It is common for wicked spirits to produce these effects to disturb, harass, and cause fear. For such cases, I suggest this pattern prayer:

Great sovereign God and Father of the Lord Jesus, we come to You in the authority You have granted in Christ. We ask You to remove the presence and activity of wicked spirits from our house and command them to go where the Lord Jesus sends them. If there is some reason why they claim the right to harass us in this place, we ask You to reveal that to us so that we might remove the cause---whether it be sin, some event, some practice, or some object in the house that the enemy claims as moral ground.

We dedicate any offending object to You, Lord, and ask to lead us to the object to dispose of it. If some demon-driven event took place herein, we as present owners or residents cancel that ground and command any demons to leave in Jesus name. If this house has been built on grounds previously used for occult or evil religious purposes, we ask You to remove evil influences. We dedicate this house to You. Sanctify it for your use only. Send your angels to guard us. If we need to know anything further, please disclose that to us. We will not fear, for You protect your own. We give You thanks in Jesus name. Amen.

Prayer for Dedicating a House or Building

Lord, You possess heaven and earth. We dedicate this place to You. Use it for your glory. Remove from it anything that offends you, objects to which demons lay claim, or curses that may have been made against it. We ask you to keep this place free from the influence or wicked spirits and to allow your people to enjoy it and to use it for your glory and the good of those who come here. In the name of the Lord Jesus we ask this. Amen.

Prayer for Spiritual Welfare of Children

According to the Bible, parents have the responsibility and privilege to care for the spiritual well-being of their children---natural or adopted (Deut. 6:1--2; Eph. 6:4). This includes protecting them from the schemes of the devil. One of the most common means of entrance to harassment of children is through the ancestral line. According to the Second Commandment God visits the iniquity of the forefathers on the third and fourth generations. This warning is connected to idolatrous worship related to false religions. In worshiping idols or in immoral behavior demons are involved and seek control (Ps. 106:34--38; 1 Cor. 10:19--20). We do not need to know the particulars of ancestral involvement in religions or ungodly activities, but we can pray for the children in their line by confession, renunciation, and command. This fits the pattern of confession by such Bible leaders as Daniel and Nehemiah. In view of the biblical warnings, examples, and responsibilities I suggest the following prayers for the welfare, safety, and freedom of children.

For Natural Children

Heavenly Father, we come in the name of the Lord Jesus Christ, our risen Savior and victor over evil, to pray as parents responsible for the spiritual welfare of our child, _____. Whatever there may be in our ancestral past---whether known or unknown---in the line of demonic, occult, or immoral involvement, this we confess it as sin and ask You to cancel the curse and the demonic claim upon us and our children. From whatever control or influence the enemy may seek to exercise we claim the freedom that You Lord God, have provided for your genuine believers. If there have been curses or spells from inside or outside the family and if there have been religious ceremonies, dedications of the descendants, bargains with the devil, immoral or violent behaviors, or any sacrifices or blood shed so as to affect descendants of the family, we as parents and as lineal members of the family and believer priests before the true and living God, break and cancel them through the Lord Jesus. Free the children from demonic activity, control, influence or conspiracy. By the Holy Spirit lead them to trust the Savior and to live lives that honor Him and experience the freedom, love, and joy that He supplies. In Jesus' name we command any demonic agents assigned to _____ to depart and go to where the Lord Jesus commands. Amen.

For Adopted Children

Holy Father, we come to You on behalf of the child we plan to adopt or have adopted. We pray for your selection of the child. As legal parents and guardians of the child's welfare we ask you to cancel the ancestral curses and influences against _____. As those You have placed in authority over this child we are claiming freedom for _____. Help us to set a godly example for him/her. We ask that he/she may come to understand the gospel of the grace of God in Jesus Christ and to trust Christ as Savior early in life and follow His plan for life. Whatever false religions and demonic connections there may be in this child's past we cancel and break in Jesus' name and ask You to free _____ from any ancestral sins and claims. This we claim in the authority granted us by our union with Christ.

If our child has been the victim of immoral, improper or violent treatment, or of ungodly religious ceremony, we ask the defeat of demonic forces against this child and the removal of such influences from this child's life. We also ask that whatever emotional damage resulted might be healed and wholeness restored. May _____ experience your love and acceptance, freedom, and joy.

Note: In praying for adopted children you may incorporate any of the petitions involved in the prayer above for natural children.

Questions to Ponder

1. Explain some of the features of the imprecatory psalms---the psalms that pray against enemies. How could you use any of these psalms as you pray?

2. What is your position in Christ and how does it affect the way you pray?

3. Which of the prayers in this chapter for personal needs seemed most relevant to you? Why?

4. Can you explain the far reaching effects of ancestral sins?

5. How do you understand the sins of your ancestors affecting you or your descendants?

CHAPTER 9

Prayer for Church and Missions

The Lord Jesus said that He would build his Church even in the face of opposition of the forces of evil (Matt. 16:18). The gates of the unseen world would not prevail against His program. The gates refer to the authorities who sat there to adjudicate matters of law and government. The unseen world is the realm of evil spirits. The Lord Jesus is sovereign and gracious. His building plan shall prevail. However, we are called to pray for the building of the Church in quantity and quality. Let me suggest several ways in which we and pray specifically.

Prayer for Revival in the Local Church

Lord, thank You for your encouraging word in Isaiah 57:14--15: "And it shall be said, 'Build up, build up, prepare the way, remove every obstacle out of the way of My people.' For thus says the high and exalted One who lives forever, whose name is Holy. I dwell on a high and holy place, and also with the contrite and lowly of spirit in order to revive the spirit of the lowly and to revive the heart of the contrite."

We seek your guidance, help, and encouragement; and You have said, "Behold, the Lord's hand is not so short that it cannot save;

neither is His ear so dull that it cannot hear. But your iniquities have made a separation between you and your God, and your sins have hidden His face from you, so that He does not hear" (Isa. 59:1--2).

So we confess our sins of omission and commission. We have not always been attentive and obedient to your Word. We have gone our own way. If this church has compromised the truth, hurt people, allowed sinful behavior to go undisciplined, we repent. We need your restoration and revival. So we claim your promise to forgive, to cleanse, and to restore. We would pray, "Answer me quickly, O LORD, my spirit fails; do not hide Thy face from me, lest I become like those who go down to the pit. Let me hear Thy lovingkindness in the morning; for I trust in Thee; teach me the ways in which I should walk; for to Thee I lift up my soul. Deliver me, O LORD, from my enemies; I take refuge in Thee" (143:7--11). We pray for ourselves individually. We pray for our assembly, for our corporate life, that it might be pleasing to you, the true and living God. Revive us and we will call upon your name. "Will You not Yourself revive us again that Thy people may rejoice in Thee? Show us Thy lovingkindness, O LORD, and grant us Thy salvation" (Ps. 85:6--7). We join Habakkuk in his prayer: "O LORD, revive Thy work in the midst of the years. In the midst of the years make it known" (Hab. 3:2).

We ask that You, Lord Jesus, would build your Church. Cause us to grow and function properly under the Holy Spirit. Help us to truly love and serve one another with a pure heart. Purify our motives, direct our decisions, and empower our outreach as we seek to win and make disciples for You.

We ask you to defeat all the schemes of Satan against us individually and as a body of believers. Remove the blinding and resistance to the gospel. Break the assignments of the devil against this church. Draw people to the trust the Lord Jesus. Help us to disciple those who come to You to build them up in the faith.

Help us to deal honestly with our sin and relationships. Open our hearts to the truth of your Word and help us walk in the light as You are in the light so we might enjoy vital fellowship with You and with one another. We submit to You, Lord; we resist the devil; cause him to flee from us (Jas. 4:7).

Thank you, Lord, for the privilege of coming to You in Jesus' authority. Thank You for your concern for us individually and for our congregation. Revive, renew, restore, revitalize us to do your will; and we will praise You. We pray in the name of the Head of the Church, the crucified, risen Savior. Amen.

Prayer for Pastors and Missionaries

I thank You, Lord God, for those You have called and appointed to help us fulfill the Great Commission. May they keep their relation to You and their interpersonal relationships clean and clear of selfish motivations and actions. Enhance their family bonding and communications. May their programs align with your purposes for Your glory. Guide them in the right way. Empower them unto every good work. Help them to meet the needs of their congregations. Protect them from the evil one and his designs against them and your people. Surround them with your protecting angels. Keep them safe and in good health. Supply their physical, emotional, and financial needs. May they trust You for their needs and not be anxious. Remove Satan's opposition in every form that the gospel may go forth clearly and powerfully. Open many hearts to receive the gospel and biblical truth. Protect those who turn from false religions to the true God and Savior from retaliation by demonic forces and from human violence. Grant freedom to the sharing of the gospel. Remove from power those who oppose the spread of the gospel. Grant openness and freedom to Christian leaders in the land in which they serve. Defeat evil leaders and groups who oppose the truth and seek to harm your people. Encourage and comfort those who have suffered loss in standing for Christ. Let your name be honored. I pray this in the authority granted to me in Christ. Amen.

Prayer against False Religions

Heavenly Father, as you have said through the apostle John in your Word that there are many antichrist spirits that have gone out into the world. In view of this, I pray that You would hinder their progress in capturing the minds of men---especially your children. Expose them for who they really are with their false and hurtful teachings and practices. Undermine their credibility and awaken people to their deceptions. Expose their false concepts of God and of man. May your truth, your true nature, and the true nature of humans whom you created in your image be recognized. Destroy the work of the devil in distorting the true nature and work of the Lord Jesus. Remove the blinding of the enemy from many eyes, convict of sin, righteousness, and judgment. Draw many to trust in the true Lord Jesus. May many recognize that He is the God-man who paid for our sins fully and completely by His death and rose again with your approval and is now at your right hand to save all those who come to You through Him. Amen.

Questions to Ponder

1. What does confession of sin have to do with renewing the spiritual life of the church?

2. What sort of needs or dangers do you think pastors and missionaries face from the enemy?

3. What do demons have to do with the promotion of false world religions? See Psalm 106:34--38.

4. What parts of the gospel message do think Satan would distort?

CHAPTER 10

Prayer for Our Country and the World

We should extend our horizons according to a biblical world view. Christ would extend His kingdom beyond our environs. He is concerned for the world around---the nations and the world.

Prayer for Our Country

I recognize, O Sovereign God that You rule over all nations. I am concerned for mine. We have strayed far from your way and have blatantly disobeyed your commands and desires. We have suffered because of this with many social, material, financial, international, and spiritual ills. I repent on behalf of my nation and ask You for your mercy and intervention. Change our hearts---those of the people and our leaders. Turn our hearts to obey Your Word and to reject evil. I pray for the three branches of our government---the executive, the legislative, and the judicial---that they would honestly and faithfully follow our constitution. I pray that they would respect human life at every stage from the womb to old age, that they would enact and support laws that protect our country and our life and maintain our freedom of speech and religion. May this country continue to exist and operate as a sovereign nation under God. Place in our government those who will support biblical views of life, liberty, and the pursuit of godliness. Move your people to exercise their rights in voicing their opinion and voting in elections. Guard the military, the law enforcement agents, and the public servants who risk their lives for our nation and individuals. Defeat Satan's plan to weaken and destroy the Christian testimony in our country. Prevent him from positioning his agents in our government to rob us of our liberties and the privilege of sharing the gospel. Continue to support your people that they may support your missionary enterprise here and around the world. Maintain our constitutional right to express our faith apart from intervention of the government. Intervene to accomplish your purpose in our country and its place in the world scene. This I pray in the name of the sovereign Savior. Amen.

Prayer regarding Human Trafficking

Human trafficking and slavery is reported as the second largest industry in the world after addictive drugs. Millions around the world are enslaved and hurting. I suggest that we could pray the following.

Holy Father, I know it breaks your heart to see those made in your image trapped in slavery and sexual bondage. In times past You have delivered your people from bondage. I know the enemy loves to enslave and torment. In Jesus' name I pray that You would break those who lead and prosper by selling humans and that You would disrupt and ruin Satan's plan to further this outrageous, inhuman practice. Prosper and strengthen those who oppose this slavery. Thank You for those agencies that already actively seek to oppose such practice and who seek to rescue men, women, girls, and boys. Raise up other organizations and services that minister to those trapped in this way. Bless those training programs and those in training for ministry in this area. Free victims from Satan's power and his agents who hold them in bondage. Heal those so mistreated and restore to them life and health. I pray in the powerful name of the Risen Lord. Amen.

Prayer for Our Educational System

Lord God, You who gave us minds and would have us learn and practice truth that benefits us and those around us, turn our educational system back to a godly basis and practice. We have long deviated from biblical truths of creation, redemption, and godly living. We have based our public education on humanistic philosophy and evolutionary presuppositions. I pray for educational leaders and teachers that they would recognize your truth as revealed in the Bible and cultivate righteous and loving attitudes and programs that will enrich our nation and promote respect and good relationships. Break the power of the devil as he continually seeks to denigrate the dignity of humans and to promote self-centered education that ignores You and your rule. Raise up those who will promote godly truth in social studies, history, math, science, and religion. We need your specific intervention badly. In Jesus name I pray. Amen.

Prayer for Christian Education

Lord Jesus, You gave us the Great Commission to make disciples, to support, and to direct those involved in Christian education. I pray for Christian grammar and high schools, for Christian colleges, for Bible schools, and for seminaries. May they stay true to your Word and to their educational purposes. Support them and guide them in selection of faculty and courses that they may promote biblical truth and discipleship. Deliver them from straying from your ways. Provide the students of your choice to train to serve You and to contribute effectively to prospering of our society and your Church. Prevent restrictions and opposition from governments from hindering their work. Cause your plan for your people and our societies to successfully establish conditions for the spreading of your truth. We ask for intervention and enablement by your Spirit. Amen.

Prayer for Governmental Leaders

Sovereign God and Father, You have established governments for the good of the people. You have told us to pray for our leaders, for kings, and those in authority. So we bring the leaders of our country to You for their blessing. Lead them in right paths---paths of justice and consideration for those they govern. Give them wisdom to execute their responsibilities to guide and uphold the laws of the land. May they look to You for guidance and support in proper administration. We pray for elected governing bodies that they would care for their constituency and the welfare of the whole country not just special groups. May they enact just and proper laws to guide our nation. We pray for the legal branch and the judges that they may have wisdom to evaluate and judge fairly and impartially. We pray by name for those we know and for those who represent our regional interests that they and their families may be kept safe. Protect all our leaders from Satan's harm and conspiracy and keep them on a straight moral path that they may fulfill properly their duties under your providential guidance. In Jesus' name I pray. Amen.

Prayer for Defeat of Ungodly Movements

There is increasing opposition from organizations, government agencies, media, and courts that oppose Christian and Biblical values and threaten the freedom of speech and expression of religion granted by our constitution. This requires specific prayer against the forces of evil behind such influences. I suggest prayers such as the following.

C. Fred Dickason, Th. D.

Father God, ruler of nations, who through your Son defeated Satan and his forces, we call for your despoiling the demonic elements that have affected and controlled those opposing your truth. Dismantle their schemes and ruin their plans to uproot and despoil your church and its testimony. Destroy their plans to remove all mention of God or Christ from public or military expression. Bring your judgment upon them. Give your children---especially those in influential positions---boldness and access to the means to stand against such evils. Deliver them from not administrating in truth and love for fear of being labeled discriminatory. We call for the defeat of organizations that undermine our God-given freedoms---such as the ACLU, Freedom from Religion Foundation, Americans United for the Separation of Church and State, and Military Religious Freedom Foundation. They would blatantly remove all reference to the Bible and Christ in our government and society. They seek judgment and removal of those who would express their religious convictions. We commit this serious concern to You and ask You to intervene for your people. In the name of the Lord Jesus we pray. Amen.

Prayer against Terrorism

Living God, how horrible are the ideologies and wretched practices of terrorists who wantonly deal out destruction and death against humans made in your image and particularly against your people! I pray that You would destroy their plans, ruin their reserves, hinder their progress, and turn many of them and their supporters to the truth in the Lord Jesus. Jesus stated that the devil is a murderer and liar from the beginning, and he is behind such terrorist movements. I ask that as many of his programs as You see fit should be brought to ruination. Judge those who would destroy your people Israel and your Church. Allow us to live in peace and safety and give our leaders and protectors great wisdom and direction in preventing and countering the actions of terrorists. Guard your people here and abroad, and heal those who have been hurt. I pray in the name of the King of Peace. Amen.

Prayer for Truth in Media

We recognize that humans involved in media often misunderstand and distort or manipulate the facts according to their own ideologies. I pray that You will override the minds of those involved in withholding or distorting their public presentations. Open the minds of the public to see the distortions and move them to seek out true information. Urge our citizens to be informed and to participate in their roles in society and government with understanding and responsibility. May your people take the lead in this determination to seek out the truth and act in responsible fashion. In Jesus' name I pray. Amen.

Prayer for Suffering Christians

There are several informational guides as to how to pray for those persecuted for the cause of Christ. Governments and false religions seek to eliminate the influence and presence of Christians worldwide. We can learn to pray for specific needs through publications of such organizations as Slavic Gospel Mission, Barnabas Aid International, and Voice of the Martyrs. Check the internet as to how to obtain pertinent publications.

We could pray to our sovereign Lord in patterns similar to the following.

O Sovereign and Gracious Lord, we ask You for your support for those who are persecuted and suffering for your name's sake. You have told us that this is our lot in this present evil age. But there are many who are suffering beyond measure---they and their children. You know who they are. We bring them before You for safety, for relief, for comfort, for encouragement, for strength to stand true to You in their trials. Uphold them with your righteous right hand. Comfort, strengthen, encourage, and heal them. Make them to know your approval and sustaining presence. Help them to live graciously forgiving those who persecute them. We come against the evil and misguided groups who violently oppose your people. Remove them as You see fit from the scene. Destroy their powers. Bring peace and institute better governments, policies, and ease the restrictions against Christian gatherings and worship. Grant that the gospel will sound out bright and clear in the midst of such havoc. Come against Satan and his agents who persecute your own. Destroy their schemes and their power. Send your angels to protect your people. May they see your power at work, repent, and turn to You. Thank You for your intervention in Jesus' name. Amen.

Prayer for the Persecuted Church

Lord Jesus, many of your people suffer at the hands of governments and false religions. We are not surprised, for You told us that this is our lot in following You. We lift up to You your hurting believers. Comfort, strengthen, encourage, and heal those who suffer for your sake. According to your will, change the hearts of the opposition. May many turn to You. Restrain the rest. Allow changes in laws and treatment of Christians that will allow them to gather and to worship freely. I pray in Jesus' name. Amen.

Prayer against Witchcraft and Satanism

We realize, holy and sovereign Lord, that You have allowed and limit the activities of false religions including witchcraft and Satanism. We pray that You will restrain their activities against your people and your Church. You are building your Church in number and in quality even in the face of the opposition of the unseen world of spirits. Protect your people from the activities, curses, and spells of these enemies. We pray against those who on the day of the full moon, at the new moons, at the equinoxes, and who at their special calendar dates meet to ask wicked spirits to carry on their programs and purposes against your people. Prevent their sacrifices and their prayers from effectiveness and send your angels among them to disrupt their proceedings. Defeat their evil intentions. Show your power to frustrate them. Bring many of them to repentance and come to Christ. Let us see your intervention in their defeat and turn many to You. We pray in the powerful authority of the crucified, risen, and exalted Christ. Amen.

Prayer for Peace

We know, Father God. that there will be no lasting peace until the Lord Jesus returns to personally reign in righteousness. He will govern with a rod of iron all the nations as a beneficent king. But until that time, be pleased to keep as much peace as pleases You and carries out your plans. Defeat the intentions and acts of terrorism where You please that your people may live in peace and witness to the gospel of peace. We pray especially for the peace of Israel, your chosen people. Protect them and prosper your grace among them. May many come to recognize the Lord Jesus as Messiah and trust Him for their personal and national well being. May your glory be known world wide. We pray in Jesus' name. Amen.

Conclusion

These are but a few suggestions that serve as patterns for your prayer in spiritual warfare. Check out the Psalms for the imprecatory prayers. Psalms 7: 10. and 28 are good examples of praying against the enemy. Learn to incorporate into your times of prayer such prayers as have been written here. You could set aside a special part of the day for serious warfare praying. You might organize groups of believers concerned for these matters to encourage each other and to pray together.

You need not cover everything that has been presented in one period of time. You can space it out, but I urge you to give yourself seriously to spiritual warfare praying. It is necessary, it is effective, it is rewarding, and it will glorify the Captain of Our Salvation.

Questions to Ponder

1. Why would Satan and demons be interested in influencing government and education? What possible evidence do you see in his involvement?

2. For what reason would spirit enemies get involved in medicine and science?

3. Research Satanism and witchcraft. What influences might they want to express?

4. List some areas in your life or in your society where you sense demonic influence.

5. How has your world view changed in light of this study? How will this affect your perceptions and your practices?

SELECTED BRIEF BIBLIOGRAPHY

The following books are recommended for their perspective and prayers in the matter of spiritual warfare praying. Not too many books deal with this sort of praying.

Bubeck, Mark I. *The Adversary*. Chicago: Moody Publications, 1975.

Bubeck, Mark I. *Preparing for Battle*. Chicago: Moody Publications, 1999.

Bubeck, Mark I. *Spiritual Warfare Prayers*. Chicago: Moody Publications, 1997.

Bubeck, Mark I. *Warfare Praying*. Chicago: Moody Publications, 2016

Dickason, C. Fred. *Angels, Elect and Evil*. Chicago: Moody Publications, 1995.

Dickason, C. Fred. *Demon Possession and the Christian*. Formerly Wheaton, IL: Crossway Books, 1987, and now Amazon.

Foster, Neill Foster. *Sorting Out the Supernatural*. Camp Hill, PA: Christian Publications, 2001. (distinguishing the false from the true)

Logan, Jim. *Reclaiming Surrendered Ground*. Chicago: Moody Publications, 1995.

McBride, Kathryn. *A Warrior's Prayerbook*. Chicago: Letcetera Publishing, 2014. (compilation of several author's prayers)

Payne, Karl I. *Spiritual Warfare: Christians, Demonization and Deliverance*. Sammamish, WA: Cross Training Press, 2004.

Warner, Marcus. *R.E.A.L. Prayer: A Guide to Emotional Healing*. Carmel, IN: Deeper Walk International, 2011.

Warner, Marcus. *What Every Believer Should Know about Spiritual Warfare*. Carmel, IN: Deeper Walk International, 2009.

ORGANIZATIONS THAT PROMOTE SPIRITUAL WARFARE PRAYER

Biblical Restoration Ministries
1551 Indian Hills Dr., Suite 200
Sioux City, IA 51104
(712) 277-4760

C.A.R.E.
9731 South M-37
Baldwin, MI 49304
(231) 745-0500

Deeper Walk International
13295 North Illinois St.
Carmel, IN 46032
(877) 467-4222

Northwest Biblical Counseling Center
P.O. Box 59025
Renton, WA 98058
(425) 687-4874

Restoration in Christ Ministries
P.O. Box 479
Grottoes, VA 29441
(540) 249-9119

Lydia Discipleship Ministries
P.O. Box 62069
Colorado Springs, CO 80962
www.lydiadm.org

CPSIA information can be obtained
at www.ICGtesting.com
Printed in the USA
JSHW041200200522
26053JS00002B/73